ANCIENT SECRETS OF SOFT SKILLS UNRAVELLED

ANCIENT SECRETS OF SOFT SKILLS UNRAVELLED

Uday Shankar

BLOOMSBURY

NEW DELHI • LONDON • OXFORD • NEW YORK • SYDNEY

BLOOMSBURY INDIA
Bloomsbury Publishing India Pvt. Ltd
Second Floor, LSC Building No. 4, DDA Complex, Pocket C – 6 & 7,
Vasant Kunj, New Delhi, 110070

BLOOMSBURY, BLOOMSBURY INDIA and the Diana logo
are trademarks of Bloomsbury Publishing Plc

First published in India 2021
This edition published 2021

ISBN: PB: 978-93-54350-57-3; eBook: 978-93-54350-62-7
2 4 6 8 10 9 7 5 3 1

Typeset in Manipal Technologies Limited
Printed and bound in India

MIX
Paper from
responsible sources
FSC® C016779

CONTENTS

PREFACE

Karma follows you wherever you go—from the past to the present, from birth to death, from youth to old age and from campus life to the corporate world. However, it is not right to put the entire burden of the journey our life takes on karma.

Karma gives us a canvas called life, not one or two but 70 years to learn and practice skills that will empower us to face the challenges of life.

Soft skills have been in existence since time immemorial and history bears testimony to their efficacy in dealing with a range of situations. In the modern world that we inhabit, soft skills can make a difference to our quality of life and help us succeed in our endeavours to scale newer heights. In this book, I have kept management jargon to a bare minimum and tried to motivate readers through stories and anecdotes while making reading an enjoyable experience.

I believe that real-life experiences teach us some of the best lessons in life. I am inspired by our epics like the Ramayana and the Mahabharata, as also the teachings of Buddha, which are more relevant now, especially in the volatile, uncertain, complex and ambiguous world of today.

Known as life skills and soft skills in modern parlance, this book will bring alive a range of skills and strategies dating back to centuries, skills that are as relevant today when it comes to facing challenges.

The book covers a range of topics from communication skills, empathy and behavioural aspects to relationships, leadership and the art of getting along with people. The narrative is interspersed with stories of yore, anecdotes and from the lives of great men, and the language is simple. Each chapter has an important takeaway.

Life skills are a necessity and should be acquired early on to enable the development of a well-rounded personality, giving you a distinct edge over others.

I dedicate this book to our brave soldiers who defend our motherland day in and day out, sacrificing everything so that a lesser mortal like me can write and try to make a difference to the lives of others.

I

Courtesy and Manners

> 'You may not do business with them. The least that you can do is, treat them with courtesy for they can always come back.'

This was back in the days when I was working in Tokyo. Searching for a vegetarian restaurant serving quintessentially Indian cuisine was a big challenge. Finally, I found one in Shinjuku, a suburb that was a 25-minute train ride from where I was staying. Every evening, I would come back to the hotel where I had been put up, have a wash and take the train to Shinjuku for dinner.

The owner of the restaurant was a young Japanese man who was deeply interested in India and its cuisine. I became one of his regular customers and he too took a special interest in me, to the extent that on Diwali, he made sure to lay out an irresistible spread of gulab jamuns, kheer and parathas for me. Needless to say, I never missed an opportunity to visit his restaurant.

One evening, I finished my dinner and was about to leave when it started pouring. The station was a good 10 minutes away and I would have been soaked had I tried to venture out. Seeing that I was stuck, the owner went outside and returned with an umbrella. Then he asked his assistant to man the counter and holding the umbrella in his hand, he walked me all the way to the station and made sure I got onto the train. It was an incredibly courteous gesture on his part, one for which I thanked him profusely. Throughout my career, I have worked and interacted with people across the globe but nowhere have I seen anyone as courteous and humble as the Japanese. The Land of the Rising Sun truly embodies humility and hospitality.

It, however, rankles me to no end when I find the absence of such behaviour and etiquette in my own country. There are several reasons for that. As soon as India attained Independence, the focus shifted to the importance of education. The statesmen and leaders at the helm of affairs rightly gave English its place in a newly independent nation. However, there wasn't much emphasis on etiquette and manners in the formative years; especially at the school and college level. In what can be termed as an unfortunate gaffe since Independence, the founding fathers of independent India never thought of introducing etiquette, manners and behaviour in the curriculum. In school, morning classes would start with a prayer and the national anthem would be sung on special days. In the 1960s, moral science was introduced as a subject, but that didn't quite address social behaviour—so essential for students in their formative years. In this context, it would be worth mentioning that George Washington, long before he became the first president of USA (1789–1797), wrote the book *Rules of Civility & Decent Behaviour in Company and Conversation* at the age of 16. The book features 110 rules which shaped the way Americans would think and conduct themselves.

The statesmen in India would have done well to take a leaf out of George Washington's approach. He seemed to have thought deeply about how one should carry oneself in the interactions with people. This compendium practically covered every aspect of human behaviour in public and was worth emulating irrespective of geography, culture or creed.

Good manners, when inculcated in children in their formative years, leave a lasting impression. As the child grows up, s/he becomes a well-rounded individual, giving the person a distinct edge over others. I can say from first-hand experience that childhood lessons are critical. I was barely six months old when my father obtained a two-year scholarship to study dairying at the Massey Agricultural College, New Zealand, after which he returned and settled down in a government job. During his stint abroad, he learnt a lot and taught me a few lessons which I remember to this day.

As a schoolboy, I would get my clothes pressed along with the tie. One day, he noticed that I hadn't polished my shoes. He bought a Cherry Blossom shoe polish—a popular brand in those days—and spent five minutes polishing them till I could see my reflection in their surface.

'People will look at your shoes first,' he said.

On another occasion, he taught me restroom manners.

'When you use the toilet, leave it in the same condition it was in when you entered.'

The best part of the explanation was the demonstration. He set about working with the brush, cleaner and bucket and in a matter of minutes, the transformation was complete—leaving the commode sparkling and bright. Those were my first lessons on washroom etiquette, which I follow diligently even now. Keeping the room clean was the next lesson in his long list of etiquette and manners.

'The moment you get up, make your bed. This should be your first task in the morning—it gives you a feeling that you have started the day on a clean slate.'

These lessons have stayed with me to this day, so much so that when I travel for business and stay at hotels, I instinctively make my bed as soon as I get up, even as the housekeeping staff rub their eyes in total disbelief. No wonder, it is said that the lessons learnt in childhood are lessons learnt for life.

At school, I vividly remember my English teacher telling the class, '"Please" and "thank you" are the small changes you pay to get along with people in life.'

Courtesy and manners go hand in hand and might well be the deciding factors when it comes to a promotion or, for that matter, even a business deal. Manners make a man; position and pelf don't.

Quite often, you come across highly educated professionals who display a lack of manners and civic sense. In the early 2000s, I was working for an information technology (IT) giant in Hyderabad. One day, as I was driving to my office, a young man who was at the wheel of a mid-sized car overtook me. As he whizzed by, I could see his company sticker on the rear windshield. A few minutes later, I caught up with him at the signal, which had turned red. He was trying to rush through but was promptly reprimanded by the traffic policeman on duty. He grudgingly pulled back. His uncouth behaviour didn't end there. He pulled down the window and spat out the juice of the paan[1] he was chewing. The light turned green and unfortunately, his bad behaviour still wasn't done. As I followed him, he offloaded a consignment of potato chips close to the divider. Finally, an empty mineral water bottle was flung out of the window, bringing an end to an unsavoury drama.

One of the questions I am often asked is—how do we learn manners? My one-word answer is 'observation'. What books, stories, lessons and lectures don't teach us, observation does. I noticed, in Japan, courtesy always begins with the other man. On one occasion, my host, who was in charge of the hospitality department of one of Japan's top electronics companies with which the Indian company I represented had dealings, had invited me for dinner. There were quite a few representatives from local Japanese companies who were also invited. They were all standing and resumed their seats only after the guests sat down. It was no different when I would get into an elevator. Knowing fully well that I was a foreigner, they would always make way for me before entering the lift. Courtesy and manners are manifestations of relationship building both at personal and professional levels. Many companies go out of the way to make customers comfortable; business is the last thing on their mind. It is no rocket science to understand that the right demeanour, or the lack of it, has a bearing on the image of the company.

Closer home, Mumbai, as always, is a vibrant city full of opportunities and a good place to rise quickly

[1] Paan betel leaf.

in the corporate world. It was early 2000 and I was looking for a change. I received a call from a company that belongs to one of India's top business houses for an interview for a senior management position.

I went at the appointed hour and was received by the human resources (HR) manager. Within a few minutes, I was led to the office of the company's vice president, who greeted me warmly. The meeting lasted for an hour and a half. It was time for lunch and the host took me to the executive lunchroom where a generous spread awaited us. Soon after, when it was time for me to leave and the taxi was waiting at the door, the vice president personally came down to see me off.

Though the job didn't come my way, I still remember the company and the people for their exemplary manners, courtesy and professional behaviour. I have attended quite a few interviews in my career but this was one of those interviews I would never forget despite not getting the job.

What matters is the way you treat people, not what you offer.

Why are people casual and disrespectful to others? If we delve deep into their psyche, it is evident that these people lack emotional intelligence and show immaturity not consistent with their age and status. As a result, success would have eluded them on a number of occasions. Such people have low self-esteem and are never at peace with themselves or, for that matter, with others. Instead of improving their communication and relationship-building skills, they continue their rude behaviour. For them, there will inevitably come a time when they are shunned by friends, society and well-wishers and find themselves all alone. The quicker they fix their attitude, therefore, the better for them; else, discourtesy and boorish behaviour can wreak havoc and cause irreparable damage to a person's career in particular and their life in general.

Another cause of such behaviour is a person's ego. To some extent, mistakes, gaffes and incomplete information are tolerated in the business world but not incivility. For all you know, the customer may never visit you again if s/he feels slighted.

In the business world the giver–acceptor relationship is of paramount importance where courtesy and polished behaviour can always draw the prospect towards you a second time.

How do you react when faced by such people at a time when you least expect it? Professionals in the sales and marketing functions face myriad situations in their daily life; some pleasant while others worth forgetting. I came across a young professional who was downcast. I asked him the reason and he told me that his client with a friendly demeanour, who usually spoke to him cordially, lost his temper and yelled at him. He confessed to me that given a choice, he would never visit the client again. There is nothing uncommon about incidents as the one above, which should be seen as a part and parcel of daily life. Every person has a bad day at the office due to various reasons, ranging from personal to professional. If you go back in time, the same person would have given you repeat orders over the years. One swallow doesn't make a summer. Give him another chance. If the same attitude persists even in a second interaction, it would be worth the while forgetting the party and moving to other prospects. However, there is no guarantee that the next man you meet would be courtesy personified; from the frying pan into the fire. However, this is easier said than done, particularly for executives in sales and marketing jobs, who do not have the luxury of walking out looking at the business potential when competitors are breathing down their necks.

One strategy would be to draw them away from the real subject to something light-hearted and disconnected from business. Talk about cricket, politics and a few other subjects under the sun. Gauge their interest and seize the moment when seriousness gives way to a smile. Continue the conversation until their nerves are settled and then introduce the subject for which you are there.

In business, the 'meeting fire with fire' approach does not work.

In the years I had spent in the technology industry, I noticed a rather strange pattern of behaviour among the so-called seasoned professionals. Vendors and service providers were made to wait for long hours even after fixing appointments. After a cursory hearing not lasting more than 10 minutes, my colleagues would excuse themselves on the pretext of getting into a meeting when in reality, none was scheduled.

At the outset, we must realise that sales executives come for business and not for charity. You might have the upper hand as a customer but that doesn't give you the right to waste their time or treat them in a lackadaisical manner.

Treating sellers with courtesy is a fine example of professional behaviour. Once you put them at ease, they open up, sharing information easily, giving you rare insights into their products and the concomitant solutions you have been looking for.

Very few professionals in the corporate world realise that vendors and sellers are great resources for information and networking. Since they know the market well, they can get you up to speed on current trends, new products, technologies and cost-saving measures that will positively impact your company.

Let me share with you yet another unforgettable experience, a veritable lesson in courtesy from the Land of the Rising Sun.

One sunny day in Japan, I hailed a cab for a short journey. In a bid to take a short cut, the driver entered a one-way lane, just broad enough for a single car to pass. The lane was a good 100 metres long and by Japanese standards, quite congested. I was sitting next to the driver and noticed a lady walking in the middle of the road, right in front of the cab.

The driver slowed down the cab, turned off the AC and followed the lady keeping a distance of over a 100 feet from her. After a few minutes, the lady turned back and realised that she was blocking the road. She very apologetically hurried to the sidewalk. The driver didn't use the horn once as it would have disturbed her.

Japanese society, to a great extent, is deeply influenced by Shinto religious beliefs, where humility and compassion are tenets that are accepted and practised by people at large. Early on in life, children are taught social manners and harmonious co-existence by their parents. It's no wonder then that good manners have percolated so completely into the way of life in Japanese society.

Courtesy costs you nothing, but what you get in return is immeasurable.

2

Commitment: A Way of Life

> ❛The quality of a person's life is in direct proportion to their commitment to excellence, regardless of their chosen field of endeavor.❜
>
> —*Vince Lombardi*

A top executive of a US-based company was visiting Japan for the first time. He had several business meetings with his Japanese counterparts over possible collaborations and business tie-ups. He was staying at a hotel in Shinjuku, a fashionable suburb of Tokyo, bustling with commercial activity. After wrapping up work for the day, he would go around savouring the sights and sounds of the city, which had much to offer to the visitor. A week later, it was time to leave and his flight was departing at 2 AM, an ungodly hour for any traveller. Narita International Airport (NIA) was an 80-minutedrive from Shinjuku. The American executive booked a cab and left instructions with the driver to reach the hotel by 11:45 PM.

After an early dinner in a restaurant in Shinjuku, he reached his hotel and switched on the TV. From the breaking news that was flashing on practically every channel, he realised that the taxi union of Japan had decided to go on a flash strike. Their demands had not been met for a long time. Protracted negotiations between the union and the management failed to yield results as both parties were nowhere near a consensus. As a result, cab services throughout the city were suspended for the next 24 hours. As if that wasn't bad enough, the heavens opened up and it began pouring heavily, showing no sign of abating. The executive waited for the taxi till 11 PM. The tension was getting to him as he had to get back to the USA in time for an important meeting the following day. Time was running out. Away from home, in the dead of the night in a strange land, he felt a sense of helplessness stealing over him. The executive decided to walk to the nearest station and take a train to the airport. Fully drenched, he made little progress. It was 11:45 PM. As he continued to walk on the street, a car suddenly pulled up near him. The driver waved his hand and gestured to him. For a moment, the executive thought that a good soul was offering him a lift in his private car. The man at the wheel opened the door and asked him to get in. He was the driver of the cab company. Since the strike was on, he decided to bring his car and drop the executive to the airport.

People who succeed in business are committed individuals. In the service industry, just a single dissatisfied customer against a hundred satisfied ones can still sully the image of the company. The driver of the cab company in Japan focused on finding a solution rather than giving in to the problem. He had a plan B to work on in the event of an exigency. He knew full well that the prestige of the company was at stake and did everything in his capacity to honour the commitment.

The time I spent in Japan taught me more than I had learnt in the 20 odd years I worked in the corporate world across verticals. Back home, there were numerous instances of vendors and suppliers reneging on contractual commitments where I was at the receiving end of criticism from a dissatisfied management and cut a sorry figure before the management. I distinctly remember a case where capital equipment like microwave radio terminals used for communicating between offices needed to be purchased. The equipment had to be sourced from outside India. Due to shipment delays, the project got delayed by a good three months, drawing the ire of the management. The supplier had not factored in the unforeseen delay. Had he done that, I would have been spared of the embarrassment. In the summer of 2018, a lady wanted to meet me to discuss a business proposal. It was decided that we meet at 11 AM at the appointed place. I was there 10 minutes early. An hour later, there was no sign of the lady nor did she think it appropriate to leave a message. And this to discuss a conversation that was initiated by her.

The culture of Japan revolves around humility. Do not be surprised if you hit a pedestrian while cycling and s/he is the first to apologise. They also avoid saying no to the extent possible. This very act symbolises their positive culture and an approach where they would like to address every problem with hope rather than despair.

Amenability and accommodation are the skills that have turned Japan into a five trillion-$ economy even in these depressing times and ranked third in the world behind the US and China.

Back in Tokyo, I was working for one of the country's largest digital electronics company engaged in process control systems, which monitors oil-and-gas-flow parameters and helps control the process within prescribed limits. The same system had to be implemented back home in India at the country's premier oil terminal in Uran near Navi Mumbai. I was staying on the fifth floor of a hotel that afforded a panoramic view of the city. On the day I arrived, I remember asking the room service for a glass of water and the lady promptly replying that the tap water in the room was the best I could get for drinking. One night after dinner, I looked out of the window and saw a policeman standing in the middle of the road directing traffic. The road was undergoing repair and an asphalt-spewing truck was fixing potholes. It was nearing 10 o'clock and after that cursory glance out of the window, I hit the sack. I woke up sometime around 2 AM feeling thirsty and had a glass of water. As I walked towards the window and parted the blinds, what I saw took my breath away. The policeman was still there, ramrod straight, directing traffic with as much vigour in the wee hours of the morning as he had earlier in the night.

In Japanese society, 'group' is more important than 'individual', and the nation always comes first. When you leave the shores of your land and work in a foreign country, it is the best form of education you can get. As you observe their culture and their way of life, your horizons widen. A catholic view and an all-embracing approach takes precedence over the mundane.

They did as they were committed to.

Commitment and dedication to duty is rare among professionals. For those who immerse themselves in the task at hand, everything else takes a back seat. I was once invited to attend a get-together with old friends; we were all meeting after a gap of many years. The changes wrought about my time made recognition difficult. A few of them had even flown to India for the occasion. Among the mix were engineers, doctors, builders, professors and businessmen. The terrace-top party was in full swing. Quite a few people present knew that I was a singer and I was asked to open the proceedings. An honour worth accepting, I started the evening singing numbers from old films. Then it was the turn of poets to regale the audience with poetry and ghazals. It was a metamorphosis of sorts as serious professionals by day turned into entertainers by night. My classmate from school was applauded for every line of the poem he was reciting. He had specially composed poems with the theme of reunion in mind. A practising doctor who ran a hospital in the city, he had made a name for himself as a successful surgeon. What made him stand apart from others was his down-to-earth attitude and humility, unaffected by the trappings of success. The setting sun provided the perfect backdrop even as the all-pervading camaraderie characterised the proceedings of the soirée.

Nobody wanted to leave what was turning into a memorable reunion. Suddenly, as my doctor friend was reciting his third poem, his phone started ringing.

One look at the display and it was clear that the call was from the hospital.

He excused himself and went to a corner to answer. As it turned out, the patient he had operated the previous day had developed complications. His condition was worsening by the hour. It was an emergency and he had to rush to the hospital. He profusely apologised to everyone present and left the party, which continued without him; though his absence was felt by everyone there. He called me the next day and told me that the patient was doing fine, thanks to his timely intervention the night before. Though he missed the party, his commitment to his profession saved a life and brought joy to someone else's life.

This kind of commitment may make you wonder what such people are made of. The emotional make-up of a dedicated individual reveals a host of qualities. Committed people are very passionate about their job. Rain or thunderstorm, nothing ever comes in the way. I have frequently seen street painters spending hours and hours drawing sketches immersed in a riot of colours. Their unwavering focus on the subject produces a masterpiece that tells a story even as feelings and emotions come alive. A mesmerised passer-by throws a fleeting glance but keeps coming back to the canvas. A silent conversation takes place between the two at a spiritual level, a karmic experience to say the least.

Commitment starts with the self. For instance, let's take the case of smoking. I have seen many people trying to kick the habit, making promises to never light another cigarette. And just when you think that they have finally bid goodbye to the cancer stick, they invariably fall off the wagon and move back to square one and a habit that unfortunately resumes with reinforced vigour. What we need to ask ourselves when a relapse like this happens, is whether they, while promising to give up smoking to their near and dear ones, were as committed to it themselves and were not just making a promise for the sake of others. When you make a commitment to yourself, it is a test of your true character and resolve. As the saying goes—you can cheat others but you cannot cheat yourself. Committed persons are unaffected by extraneous circumstances and achieve their objective. They do not offer excuses and reach their goals even under the most adverse conditions.

Many years ago, I was working in Hyderabad. I had a special love for the city of pearls, where I was born and brought up. Other than its cosmopolitan culture, the city is known for theatre, art and music. The sprawling bungalows in the posh Banjara Hills neighbourhood with rock formations are a rare sight savoured by visitors and connoisseurs alike. Inside one such bungalow is a place called Lamakaan. The brainchild of Ashar Farhan and Humera Ahmed, the house, belonging to their late uncle M. Hasan, was transformed into a vibrant cultural space in 2010, complete with a 500 square-yard outdoor stage, a seating area and a canteen. Theatre lovers throng to watch plays by local groups like Nishumbita and Sutradhar. It was around September and I went there to watch a play. The open-air theatre housed over a hundred people and was the favourite haunt of theatre buffs.

As the tea and snacks counter closed at 7 PM, the attendees settled in their seats for an enjoyable evening.

The skies were clear and there didn't seem to be any possibility of rain. Nature, however, had other plans; it started to rain 20 minutes into the play, which was then shifted indoors as people crammed into a hall to watch the show. However, nothing could diminish the spirit of the performers as they picked up from where they had left off. The same vigour and enthusiasm was there for all to see. Just as the crowds had settled down, the lights went off leaving the place in total darkness. After waiting for nearly half an hour, the show started again as power was restored. This time, the troupe, unfazed by disruptions, completed their performance. The audience gave them a standing ovation. The big takeaway of the evening was their sheer commitment to the play—and to the audience who had come to watch them perform. Not once did they think of abandoning the play and came back stronger after every interruption. Neither rain nor a power cut had diluted their focus.

Committed individuals carry a certain amount of responsibility and are fully aware of the fact that others are dependent on them. They carry the hopes and aspirations of other people on their shoulders. They know that if let down once, the same people will not trust them a second time.

The operator of a private railway firm that serves the Tokyo suburbs issued an apology after one of its trains departed 20 seconds ahead of schedule. Passengers boarding Tuesday's 9:44:40-Tsukuba Express from the Minami–Nagareyama station, just north of Tokyo, were unaware that something was amiss when the train which had arrived on time, pulled away from the platform at 9:44:20 AM. The train's operator believed the goof-up was serious enough to warrant an apology.

'We deeply apologise for the severe inconvenience imposed upon our customers', was what the Metropolitan Intercity Railway Company said in a statement. The train's conductor had not properly checked the train's timetable, the firm said, adding that the crew had been instructed to strictly follow procedure to prevent a recurrence. Passengers who missed the train that left ahead of schedule suffered little inconvenience as the next one arrived just four minutes later. Once committed, you have to live by your word or else, do not commit in the first place. In the business world, there is always a tendency to overcommit. This is done with a view to please the bosses by getting the contract and meeting their business targets. In the rapidly evolving business world, where money is often at stake, it is better to be as realistic as possible rather than make a commitment and fail to abide by it. In the final analysis, people with commitment are most sought after. Commitment leads to consistency, which is the hallmark of an 'outperformer'. Once such individuals win the trust of others, they create a brand, an image of dependability and customer-centricity. News travels by word of mouth and soon this individual, the agency or the service becomes a household name.

Brand loyalty is built around trust, quality of service and promptness. Companies will go to any extent to protect themselves. This is precisely the reason why corporates prefer to hire committed professionals who can be entrusted with the responsibility of carving a niche for the organisation.

3

Emotional Intelligence

'How people treat you is their karma.
How you react is yours.'

—*Wayne Dyer*

In the Mahabharata, during the Kurukshetra war, the armies of the Kauravas and the Pandavas facing each other on the battlefield signified the beginning of the war between justice and injustice. Cousins who, as children, had played together and studied under the same guru were baying for each other's blood. On seeing his teachers, cousins and grandfather in the numerically superior Kaurava ranks, Arjun wilts under the burden of what he is expected to do. Fighting back tears, he says to Krishna, his charioteer in the battle, 'O Krishna. How can I kill them? They are my brothers. Over there is my grandfather Bhishma who showered love and affection on us … and my teacher Guru Dronacharya, who taught me the art of warfare.'

It is this conundrum of Arjun's that is the genesis of the *Bhagavad Gita*. Through its verses, Lord Krishna counsels Arjun to perform his duties as a warrior on the battlefield. Somewhere hidden in the narration is a lesson on emotions and emotional intelligence (EI) or emotional quotient (EQ).

Krishna explains to Arjun that his immediate task is to focus on the job at hand and not get swayed by emotions. As a warrior, he is expected to perform and deliver. Expectations are high and he must fight to win. He further goes on to explain that the battleground is not a place for emotions and he needs to go beyond filial affections and show results.

In simple terms, emotional intelligence can be described as the intelligence that is required to manage your emotions effectively with the intent of furthering a relationship. Human emotions are a response to an event or an occurrence and vary from person to person. Emotional intelligence is used to harness these emotions positively to the advantage of the individual or the organisation.

We seldom realise that EI operates at a subterranean level, whether it is in our personal interactions or professional associations. In the early 1980s and 1990s, mild interest was kindled regarding emotional intelligence—a relatively new area at that point of time. The emphasis was more on individual brilliance. Hard skills or the intelligence quotient was the sole determinant for job offers. In the mid-1990s, EI found its place under the sun, thanks largely to the pioneering efforts of Daniel Goldman, Peter Salovey and John D. Mayer. Emotional intelligence stole a march over IQ as companies started looking for well-rounded professionals who would empathise and build lasting relationships, especially in sales- and marketing-related roles where one dealt with customers. A good mix of IQ and EQ should see you through culminating in a good day at the office.

Most people tend to get emotional. However, emotions have no place at the office, but EI certainly does. In the corporate world, you meet people with a different mindset and mental make-up. Sooner or later, you will come across a person with whom you experience cognitive dissonance—someone you cannot get along with from day one. As you progress through life, a provoker lurks somewhere, one who has taken needling to an art form. How will you respond?

It was early 2000 and I was part of the senior management team of a company engaged in online trading of shares with investors and traders. It was a young company with a vibrant culture and was talked about highly in corporate circles as well as the media. After eight long years, the managing director (MD) retired and a new one took over. The latter had spent all his life in the public sector and his style of functioning was at variance with the prevailing work culture. The MD and the deputy MD had a diametrically opposite approach to work and as days progressed, the gulf between the two widened. There were frequent exchanges between them. Matters took a turn for the worse when both were involved in a heated exchange in a review meeting. Screaming at the top of his voice, the deputy MD threw a file on the table and stormed out of the meeting. Not to be outdone, the MD, an old warhorse, isolated him and started taking decisions on his own. The fissure resulted in the formation of two distinct camps. Politics replaced productivity. The ramifications were felt as many officers in the middle management left the company in search of greener pastures. In a few months, the company's leadership status eroded and the goings-on were soon in the public domain.

It was clear that at such a senior level, the emotional intelligence was lacking. Empathy, support, understanding and accommodation, which are elements of EI, were sorely missing. It is not enough to hire a team of brilliant professionals. Egos, inflexible positions and brinkmanship are the bane of any organisation. All these are a result of low emotional intelligence.

When the elephants fight, the grass under their feet suffers the most.

World leaders like Martin Luther King Jr, Nelson Mandela and Mahatma Gandhi were always calm and composed even in the face of provocation. Leaders listen to their followers, empathise with them, offer their support and ultimately solve the problem. Emotional intelligence is the basic foundation on which leadership attributes are built. Qualities like empathy, equanimity, stoicism and above all, a philosophical approach to life are aids to develop emotional intelligence. There is no better way to exemplify EI than the story of Buddha and the angry young man.

Buddha and his retinue of monks were passing through a village. Travel-weary, he chose to rest beneath a tree. Soon word spread around about the visiting teacher, leading to many villagers gathering around Buddha to listen to his words of wisdom.

Amongst the surging crowds was a young man who was of the opinion that teachers and preachers were conmen out to fleece the gullible public. Anger writ large on his face, he shouted at Buddha, 'I can see the ulterior motive behind these sermons! You are trying to fleece the villagers of their humble possessions and make money. Go back to where you came from'.

Buddha remained calm. Exuding a feeling of love and compassion, he addressed the young man. 'If you purchased a lovely gift for someone, and that person did not accept the gift, to whom does the gift then belong?'

The question rattled the young man, but he replied, 'The gift would still be mine because I was the one who bought it.'

'In the same way, I have not accepted your abuses and that is the reason why I neither get angry nor feel insulted. Your abuses are still with you.'

Anger is a punishment you give yourself for someone else's mistake. Never reply when you're angry. Never make a promise when you're happy. Never make a decision when you're sad. The man who conquers his anger, conquers the world. In the words of poet and philosopher Ralph Waldo Emerson, 'Every minute you are angry, you lose sixty seconds of happiness.'

India's first deputy prime minister Sardar Vallabhai Patel took up the onerous task of integrating 565 self-governing princely states with the Union of India. A tough assignment though it was, Sardar Patel's astute and no-nonsense approach culminated in these states getting released from British suzerainty and becoming a part of the India. Patel was a man with a steely resolve with no outward display of emotions. He believed in solving a problem and coming up with a result—a trait that earned him the sobriquet of the 'Iron Man of India'. His no-nonsense approach earned him accolades, though there were quite a few detractors who did not approve of his strong-arm methods to subdue opponents. The delay would have cost the nation dearly had it not been for Sardar Patel, who used a mix of aggression and diplomacy to achieve the impossible.

Patel, who belonged to the state of Gujarat, practised law and attended to cases in the courts of Anand, Godhra and Borsad. In 1909, his wife, Jhaverba, fell ill and was diagnosed with intestinal problems. An immediate surgery was required as the growth was malignant. Jhaverba was admitted to the hospital. She was too weak to withstand the rigours of surgery. The operation was postponed to give her time to recover and gain strength. After staying with her for some time, Patel rushed to Anand to defend his client in the court. Soon after, his wife's condition took a turn for the worse and there was no other option but to go ahead with the surgery. The operation seemed to be successful and the result was encouraging; a wire was sent to Patel at Anand informing him of the facts. A somewhat reassured Patel then started to cross-examine a key witness. As he was in the middle of cross-examining the witness, he received another telegram containing the news of his wife's demise. The moment he opened it, he knew that it wasn't good news. His wife had passed away. He quietly folded the paper, put it in his pocket and continued to hammer away until the witness broke down. Eventually, he went on to win the case.

Later, he broke the sad news to others in the court. A fine testimony of equanimity, stoicism and above all, a lesson in keeping emotions under control in the most trying times.

In the several years that I have spent in the corporate world, I have witnessed boardroom meetings turn into 'bored' room meetings. Arguments over issues would result in slanging matches often culminating in the exhibition of raw vocal power. It is difficult to control your emotions at the workplace when the pressures of the job are high.

There is no single pattern of behaviour that is exhibited. When an employee gets a promotion, s/he can hardly contain their excitement. Going from cabin to cabin, they break the news all over the office. On the contrary, not getting a promotion is bad news. S/he quickly leaves the office, avoiding colleagues offering commiserations.

At the office, it is business first and emotions later. At the end of the day, you are measured in terms of deliverables. Emotions are internal and can't be proffered as an excuse. Are emotions limited to outbursts and body language? Not really. One can't emphasise enough on the power of words, which brings into focus written communications. Right from love letters to pink slips, every communication carries an emotion. At the office, email communications are used to enhance productivity and convey the right message minus emotions. When I was working as a member of the senior management at a major IT company in Mumbai, a minor disagreement over an issue led to a heated exchange between the heads of a business unit and the support service unit. It didn't stop there. What followed was a series of the unsavoury emails between the two, involving intemperate language, usage of oversized fonts with words highlighted in flaming red. In addition to this, the two managers, who were low on EI, marked copies to all and sundry, washing dirty linen in public. The management took a serious view and both the senior executives were given a dressing down. In this case, the unsavoury episode was drawn to a close, thanks largely to the timely intervention of the management. But worse things have happened. Words, written or spoken, have a way of spiralling out of control. It was, indeed, words that almost cost Abraham Lincoln his life!

> *When dealing with people, remember you are not dealing with creatures of logic, but with creatures of emotion.*
>
> — *Dale Carnegie*

When a person comes to your office as a service provider or a product seller, s/he is coming for business, not for alms. They deserve the same kind of respect that you expect when you go to a company and offer your services. They too get annoyed and upset when you make them wait for an hour before eventually meeting them.

But what happens when you are at the receiving end? What we forget is the fact that people remember your actions and will be waiting for the first opportunity to get even with you. In either case, both lack EI. At the outset, EI teaches you to put yourself in the shoes of the other person. Empathy is a quality that will propel you to a position of acceptability. You wouldn't have imagined in your wildest dreams that this one quality is capable of making every venture of yours an unqualified success. Incidentally, empathy is a cornerstone for EI. The World Economic Forum ranked emotional intelligence sixth in the world among the list of top 10 skills that employees will need to succeed in the workplace of the future.

How does one develop EI, which is a not just a sign of maturity, but also leadership, responsibility and large-heartedness?

I was, at a point in time, someone who would get angry at the drop of a hat and raise my voice. I thought that vocal power and aggression was the only way to get things done. A few trips abroad changed my thinking. Now when I look back, I see how unreasonable I was—all this due to a poor understanding of EI. The first lesson is to display equanimity and a calm exterior. Success and failure are cyclic. If things have not been working for you for a rather long period, remember that the law of averages is bound to kick in and you will get some positive news from some quarter or the other.

Secondly, you develop a catholic view, an all-encompassing approach where you share your joys and sorrows, success and failure with your team members. Develop a calm exterior and begin a conversation with a smile. Be true to yourself and others.

Have the capacity to absorb criticism, because no person in the world is infallible. Voice is the key to a conversation—be it personal or official—so, learn to appear warm and friendly by modulating your voice.

People with high EI are anything but unidimensional. They meet others, cultivate relationships and can diversify their work experience. In addition to being a soft-skills trainer and a motivational speaker, I am a musician who learnt music for a few years. Other than the fact that music soothes my nerves and calms the senses, I get the opportunity to entertain people wherever I go.

Like karma, EI follows you everywhere you go. Life offers a wide canvas with a spectrum of colours. It is up to you to use them and end up making the picture perfect!

4

Lateral Thinking: The New Normal

'Creativity involves breaking out of established patterns in order to look at things in a different way.'

—Edward de Bono

A rich farmer fell ill and knew that his days were numbered. He wrote a will in which he expressed his wish to divide the 17 horses he owned between his three sons in the ratio of half, one-third and one-ninth. Moments after his death, the sons started squabbling over the legacy. Compounding the matter was the fact that 17 was not divisible by either two, three or nine. They called a wise old woman to settle the dispute. The woman assessed the situation and assured them that she would visit them the following day and solve their problem. The next day, the wise lady arrived riding on a horse. The animal was made to stand along with the 17 other horses, bringing the total number of horses to 18.

The process of distribution started. She called the first son and gave him nine horses. Then it was the turn of the second son who received six horses. The remaining two horses were handed over to the third son. All parties involved were happy at the settlement.

After the mediation, the woman took her horse and went home.

Call it lateral thinking or out-of-the-box thinking, it is here to stay. In 1933, Edward de Bono, a Maltese physician and psychologist, postulated a theory that thinking based on conventional wisdom cannot provide solutions to all problems. He argued in favour of a parallel thinking process which digs deep into the recesses of the mind and offers esoteric solutions to some of the most intricate problems. Bono's 'Six Thinking Hats' is a powerful set of tools that helps people be more productive, focused and mindfully involved. Out-of-the-box thinking helps us find solutions to many intractable problems which defy conventional wisdom. The solutions are not documented in any textbook nor can you find them in the speech of a gifted orator. It happens in a moment and leaves you wondering why you did not think of it before.

As a trainer, I receive requests from companies and organisations to conduct programmes for their associates across the management cadre. In the past, the exercise would start with a telephonic conversation. Then I would send them a document with a questionnaire on the need for conducting the training along with the outcome and expectations. They would promptly fill in the information and send it back to me. Based on the information that I received, I would customise the training to meet their exacting standards.

In the course of one such enquiry, a company, after going through the training document, conveyed their satisfaction and gave the go-ahead. Now it was the turn of the commercials. A surprise awaited me.

The company which was so prompt with their replies thus far stopped communicating. I sent an email a couple of times but received no response. Then I picked up the phone and asked the training coordinator about the status of the programme. The reply to that was a succinct dismissal: 'I am sorry. The pricing is on the higher side and as such the proposal is on hold.'

It was their way of saying that they were looking for the training at a price which was not acceptable to me. The entire process consumed two months before the agonising wait came to an end. The same story was repeated with three more prospective clients. I knew that vertical thinking was not the answer and I had to think out of the box.

For the next enquiry, I sent a two-line email to the company:

'Given below is the pricing for the two-day training programme. Let me know if your company can afford the costs. Once I get your feedback, we can take it forward'.

In the above approach, which was different than the conventional one, I was able to gauge the intent of the company and their seriousness. In the process, I didn't give them any leeway to use 'pricing' as an excuse to delay and finally say no to the proposal. I believed that if they were not interested then they should reject it at the outset than make me wait for two months.

Believe it or not, I have closed quite a few proposals in quick time. This led me to think that there are more ways than one to successfully engage and close the contract. All of us had no choice but to study mathematics at school. Compared to algebra and trigonometry, I found geometry to be a challenge, what with its theorems and proofs. The Pythagoras theorem, named after the famous Greek mathematician, states that in a right-angled triangle, the square on the hypotenuse is equal to the sum of the squares of the other two sides. As students, we were given the assignment of proving the theorem. Everyone in the class would prove the theorem in their own way, which happened to be different from the others. You would be surprised to know that there are more than 360 ways of arriving at the proof, which means that there is more than one way of approaching a problem. Lateral thinking is just that and begins where vertical or logical thinking ends. Lateral thinking probes into the inner recesses of your brain and brings out the creativity in you along with new ideas. It goes beyond known boundaries and allows you to stretch your thinking until a solution is found.

Conventional or vertical thinking moves in one direction. Lateral thinking moves in many directions. Vertical thinking moves only if there is a direction in which it can move. Lateral thinking 'moves' to generate a direction. Lateral thinking shifts the goalpost significantly, igniting your creativity and redefining borders. As you leave the comfort zone, you look at the problem from a new perspective. This applies across a variety of fields, from aircraft and motorcycles to technology. Stealth-bomber designers, for instance, have been inspired by the hawk and its spectacular aerobatics.

To go so far as to say that lateral thinking was used to solve problems in the Biblical days is no exaggeration. What better example than King Solomon, the wise monarch who ruled Israel between 970 and 931 BCE. Hailed by one and all, the dispassionate ruler was known to dispense justice which became an example to follow centuries after his death.

One day, King Solomon was hearing a case involving two prostitutes. The two women had both given birth to sons and they lived together in the same home. During the night, one of the infants was smothered to death. The woman whose son had died, switched her dead baby with the baby of the other woman as she slept. The other woman, seeking justice, took the matter before the king. She stated her case: 'We were alone; there was no one in the house but the two of us. During the night this woman's son died because she lay on him. So she got up in the middle of the night and took my son from my side while I, your servant, was asleep. The next morning, I got up to nurse my son—and he was dead! But when I looked at him closely in the morning light, I saw that it wasn't the baby I had given birth to.'

Solomon could not tell from their words which woman was telling the truth. Instead, he issued a shocking command: 'Bring me a sword. I will cut the living child in two and give half to one and half to the other.'

After listening to the king's pronouncement, the woman whose son was still alive said,

'Please, my lord, give her the living baby! Don't kill him!' However, the other woman, whose son had died, answered, 'Neither I nor you shall have him. Cut him in two'. Based on their responses, Solomon knew the identity of the true mother:

'Give the living baby to the first woman. Do not kill him; she is his mother'.

Why would Solomon give such an outrageous command? Did he really intend to cut a baby in half with a sword? Solomon's sole intention was to discover the truth. He did so by watching the responses of the two women and relying on the maternal instincts of the true mother. It may have been an unorthodox method, but it provided a solution to the problem where all other approaches would have failed. Solomon was no legal luminary nor did he have recourse to books on law. Yet he found the solution. In modern-day parlance, this is called lateral thinking.

There was a time when candidates appearing for an interview were asked routine questions about their experience, skills and expected salary. Today, companies are looking for creative people who can use their imagination and come up with solutions. Companies that belong to the IT, media and manufacturing sectors have to evolve and come up with new products all the time. Lateral thinking helps them stay abreast of the competition.

One of the questions thrown at the unsuspecting interviewee is:

'Can you tell us about a problem that you have solved at the workplace using lateral thinking?'

If you are prepared for this question and answer the interviewer with a real-life example, your chances of getting selected are pretty high.

How does one become a lateral thinker and what are the qualifications? Lateral thinkers are creative and want to try something which has not been tried before.

They are bold and not afraid to tread the path alone. They don't mind being made fun of. They are ready to fail but are doubly sure to succeed because lateral thinking is open-ended and offers not just one, but a range of solutions.

As a teenager, I was fascinated by James Bond and never missed any of his movies. The British agent, nicknamed 007, would devise ingenious ways of escaping from his enemies; I particularly remember the scene from the box-office hit, *Live and Let Die*. Bond is captured by his enemies and held captive in a crocodile farm from where there is no escape. Surrounded by the lethal creatures with the power of wrenching an arm or a leg in a single bite, Bond comes up trumps in the most unimaginable way. Realising that his best escape route is to use the backs of the crocodiles as stepping stones, he leaves his captors behind by doing just that. If this is not an example of lateral thinking, what is?

Greek mythology also offers a glimpse of lateral thinking—and what better example could be there than the Trojan horse! During the Trojan War, the Greeks thought out of the box and used subterfuge to enter the independent city of Troy and win the war. As per the widely told versions, after a fruitless 10-year siege, the Greeks constructed a huge wooden horse and hid a select force of men inside. They then pretended to sail away and burnt their tents. Little did the Trojans realise that the Greek army was hiding nearby and waiting to strike. The Trojans pulled the horse into their city as a victory trophy. That night, the Greek force crept out of the wooden horse and opened the gates, facilitating the entrance of the rest of the army, which had sailed back under the cover of darkness.

The Greeks swarmed all over them and destroyed the city of Troy, ending the war.

Lateral thinking comes handy at home as well. A few months ago, I was at my wit's end trying to find a solution to a problem. Two business documents had to be scanned and sent urgently. They say, lightning strikes twice and I couldn't help subscribing to the adage. Being a technology professional, nobody could understand the indispensability of a backup internet connection better than me. In addition to a cable internet connection, I had an ADSL (asymmetric digital subscriber line) dial-up link to meet any exigency. On that fateful day, both the broadband internet connections from two different internet service providers went down at the same time. Mobile in my hand, I complained and was greeted with a tardy response. It being a Sunday didn't help the cause either. Time was running out and I realised that the solution to the problem was right there in my hands—the ubiquitous cell phone. Mobile phones have a feature known as the hotspot. On activation, the phone doubles as a Wi-Fi source, providing 4G internet at a speed around 6–9 Mbps. Needless to say, the problem was solved.

Let's look at out-of-the-box thinking through *Aesop's Fables* written in 600 BCE. A thirsty crow that comes upon a pitcher with water at the bottom, which is beyond the reach of its beak. After failing to push it over, the bird drops pebbles into the pitcher one by one until the water rises to the top, allowing it to drink. The unschooled bird understood the theory of displacement of water and put it to good use. The fable shows that thoughtfulness is superior to brute strength.

In 2013, the Norwegian town of Rjukan made headlines all over the world, thanks to the ingenuity of

Martin Andersen. During the long winters, the narrow valley surrounded by mountains had to go without sunlight for six months a year. The unforgiving winters and the high ranges would plunge the town into perpetual darkness till Andersen devised a solution to the problem.

He conceived a project through a combination of public money and private sponsorship and used mirrors to reflect sunlight into the town square. Three mirrors, 17 square metres each, were brought in by helicopter and placed on a mountain wall, about 450 metres above the centre of the town. Controlled by computers, the tilted mirrors followed the course of the sun to bring sunshine to Rjukan's main square below. To the 3,400 inhabitants, life couldn't have been brighter—thanks to Andersen's lateral thinking.

In today's disruptive digital age, lateral thinking has provided innovative solutions to unsolvable problems. In its simplest form, lateral thinking holds the key when all conventional approaches have failed. It is an out-of-the-box approach not defined or limited by established laws and postulates.

In the corporate world, it is imperative to give the enduser the correct and most cost-effective solution. The problem is given to multiple groups who in turn, come out with their solutions. Participants are encouraged to think out of the box and the solution is chosen based on cost-effectiveness, long-term viability and future upgradation.

Lateral thinking is here to stay and offers a whole new dimension in problem-solving. In the days to come, it is going to be the new normal.

5

Treat People the Way You Want to Be Treated

'We come with nothing, we go with nothing,
But one great thing we can achieve in our
Beautiful life is a little remembrance
In someone's mind and a small place in someone's heart.'

—*Buddha's teachings*

Call it corporate courtesy or business etiquette, every employee in the company deserves the same amount of respect, irrespective of position or status for the simple reason that s/he is a fellow human being and has come up to that position by dint of hard work and ability. You might be in a senior position for the fact that you were well educated, knowledgeable with a hunger for learning. Never underestimate anyone you meet. Appearances are deceptive and for all you know, you may be working with a maverick capable of breaking new ground; a timeless lesson, that many of us may have heard through childhood stories.

There was once a king who was fond of playing chess. He hired experts to teach him the niceties and nuances of the game. At night, he would pour over books and make notes of tactical moves, sacrifices and the art of trapping the opponent's queen. His rise to the top wasn't meteoric but gradual. He honed his skills day in and day out and soon became a force to reckon with. He easily defeated rated players in his kingdom and the news of his skill at the game spread like wildfire. Despite his duties towards his kingdom, here was a monarch who had made a mark with his performance. Many well-known players from outside the kingdom made a beeline to showcase their skills, only to bite the dust. Outplayed and outclassed in every department of the game, the king was simply unbeatable. Soon he became the undisputed chess champion. One day, a boy barely into his teens, came to the court and sought a game with the king. On hearing the request, the entire court burst out laughing even as the derision reached a crescendo. Arrogance writ large on his face, the king said, 'Son. If you lose, will you be my servant for life?'

'Yes, Your Majesty,' replied the boy in all humility.

'If I win, all I ask you is to put a grain of rice on the 1st square, double it till the 64th and give it to me.' The wager was no big deal and the king agreed without batting an eyelid.

The table was set even as the court sat watching attentively, trying to follow every move when the match began. The boy started cautiously and soon displayed his repertoire. The king started to feel the heat as the boy, with his lightning moves, took out the king's rook and knight. A few tactical moves later, he gained control of the middle-game. A few daring sacrifices by the teenager helped his pawns advance menacingly towards the opposite flank. The beleaguered queen was well and truly trapped with no room to manoeuvre. Staring at an imminent defeat, the king resigned.

The court was stunned into silence, unable to decipher the loss.

A sackful of rice was brought and the grains were placed according to the boy's request and in the arrangement he wanted, with each successive square holding double the quantity of the previous one. To everybody's surprise, the grains of rice starting piling up and soon the required quantity was astronomically high. The king realised his mistake and rewarded the boy for his brilliance.[2]

He also learnt a valuable lesson: Irrespective of position and stature, treat everybody with courtesy and give them the respect they deserve.

More often than not, we presuppose and judge a person on his abilities without ascertaining the facts. Besides showing his prowess in the game, the boy was mature beyond his years. He was wellgrounded and knew what he was asking for. He was also aware of the fact that the king could not meet his demand as he had not pondered over the request and agreed to it in a tearing hurry.

Similar things happen in the business world. We are eager to agree to the terms and conditions of a contract without reading between the lines. We need to get a realistic understanding of the resources at hand before committing on the deliverables. Besides, it is also important to gain as much knowledge as possible about the customer, his line of business, his wins in terms of projects secured and successfully completed, his standing in the market and above all, his track record.

[2] Ancient Indian stories

Great men are unaffected by power and its trappings. I recall an interesting conversation between a bright young professional and the general manager (GM) of a company, which was told to me by a colleague. The GM was used to throwing his weight around and had a few run-ins with his younger colleague. In the course of a meeting, the senior man reminded his junior of the fact that he was speaking to the general manager of this company'.

The young man, unruffled by the authoritarian tone, told his senior that designations and power are limited to the four walls of the workplace. He went a step further and reminded his boss that at the stroke of five, they all cease to exist the moment everybody steps out of the office.

What he was suggesting was that these trappings and appendages drop off the moment you leave the workplace. We are all human first. Everything else comes later.

Nobody expects royal treatment but everybody is entitled to the bare minimum courtesy that qualifies as professional behaviour. On quite a few occasions, I have been caught without a handkerchief—thanks to my habit of losing handkerchiefs regularly. Thousands have disappeared mysteriously in what would surely deserve a mention on Ripley's Believe It or Not! I have made no effort to investigate the mystery as a couple of hosiery shops are a stone's throw away from where I live.

I picked one that was closest and made it a point to visit the shop every week. Other than handkerchiefs, I would also purchase vests, sheets and towels. Over a period of time, I noticed a marked change in the shopkeeper's attitude. I could see that he was taking me for granted for reasons better known to him. In the beginning, he would show a lot of interest, displaying a variety of items and new arrivals. Gradually, his interest waned and he hardly acknowledged my presence. I took it into my stride for some time, hoping for better customer care in the days to come. One day, the shopkeeper was showing his products to a group of ladies and was pretty engrossed. I waited for a good 20 minutes but he had no time for me. That was the final straw, and it made me realise that I needed to take my business elsewhere.

I have since zeroed in on another shop and my experience has been positive. The moment I step in, the shopkeeper welcomes me with a smile. He spends a lot of time showing me the catalogue, the designs and the new arrivals, along with the costs. What's more, he ensures that the purchases are delivered at my doorstep if the list is long. On a few occasions, he has even offered me a cup of tea. He is a kilometre away and charges 10 per cent more than the previous shop. I pay the extra money ungrudgingly, as I know that it is the price for good customer service.

While we expect others to treat us with courtesy, it is incumbent upon us to extend the same to others irrespective of who they are. On one occasion, I was to take an early morning flight to Pune and had to drag myself out of bed. The flight was due to arrive from Delhi en route to Pune. The insufferable Bengaluru winter didn't help either. The only saving grace was that the cab arrived on time. I didn't have time for breakfast or even enough time to grab a coffee. The driver greeted me with a cheery good morning as he held the door open for me and we were on our way to the airport. Half an hour into the drive, I got a message about the flight being delayed due to fog. The call for breakfast got louder, aided and abetted by the rumblings in the tummy. I requested the driver to find a good restaurant where I could have a quick bite. Drivers have an uncanny knack of finding good eateries in the area and this man was no different. Disregarding the GPS instructions, he took a detour and drove to an Udupi joint which was open for business. I dived headlong into a plate of masala dosa with a dash of butter. The first bite was sheer nirvana. After I was done eating, I chased down the fine taste with a much-needed cup of filter coffee.

Meanwhile, I asked the waiter to serve a masala dosa and filter coffee to the driver who was waiting in the cab. Once he was done, we resumed the journey and reached the airport. As I got down, he said, 'Thank you for the breakfast, sir. I enjoyed it. But this one was very special.'.

I laughed and queried, 'What is so special about it? It's the same stuff they serve day in and day out.'

'Sir, customers are so busy these days, they don't even look at us. But you made sure that I had eaten too'.

He was getting emotional, so much so that he was almost on the verge of choking. Just before leaving, he added, 'Anytime you want a cab, call me sir. I will be there.'

Small gestures make a big difference, don't they?

Companies and organisations have realised the importance of office etiquette, which invariably leads to better bonding and camaraderie among employees. It may be hard to believe but studies have shown that a friendly workplace is one of the factors responsible for greater productivity. Modern companies are pushing the 'family concept within the office'. People have realised that what is good for the heart is good for the brain. Going to office should be a pleasurable experience; it should be akin to a veritable second home where you feel at ease and put your best foot forward for the organisation.

The way you treat others is a reflection of your upbringing, your personality and your ability to carry people along with you.

History bears testimony to the fact that insults are not easily forgotten. The aggrieved party will be waiting to pay you back in the same coin at the first available opportunity. There could be no better example than Chanakya, the Brahmin and the epitome of wisdom, who was humiliated by the kings of the Nanda Dynasty, ruling over much of northern India in full view of the court.

In 371 BCE, Chanakya, who was legendary king Chandragupta Maurya's mentor, played a major role in establishing the Magadh empire which covered most of India. He played a stellar role in defeating the Nanda kings who by then had become unpopular with the masses. The ruler amassed wealth, especially gold, and was very avaricious and levied heavy taxes on peasants. Chanakya, on the other hand, was a respected scholar and mastered political science at the University of Takshashila. He was an expert in economics, warfare and politics.

However, when Magadh was under the Nanda Dynasty, Chanakya was undergoing a period of professional struggle. He was in need of a job and fortunately for him, there was a vacancy in a charity centre. King Dhana Nanda, who was at the helm of affairs, wanted a Brahmin to run the centre. Chanakya decided to apply for the position and travelled to Magadh. His insistence of a Brahmin, it was widely believed, was to restore his image; the arrogant king was not known for his hospitality and stories of his misdemeanours were doing the rounds. His reputation had plummeted and the king was keen on restoring his image.

It was said that when Chanakya entered the royal palace to apply for the position, he saw nine seats lined up in front of the throne. Eight were reserved for the Nanda princes, and the ninth chair, which was vacant, was earmarked for the incumbent centre head. Chanakya, never the one to shy away from attention, promptly sat down on the ninth seat. When King Nanda questioned his right to sit on the chair, Chanakya, a picture of confidence and authority, informed the king that he was the right candidate for the job. After all, he was a Brahmin, well versed in the Vedas and had little or no competition at that point of time. Despite his lack of dress sense, his matted hair tied in a knot, Chanakya looked at the king and spoke with conviction.

King Nanda didn't take to this kindly. A poor Brahmin reeking of arrogance didn't seem to fit the bill. He insulted Chanakya by calling him an ugly Brahmin.[3]

[3] Sastry, Rudramurty. 2011. *Chanakya* (Kannada). Bengaluru: IBH Prakashana.

Since he could not accept Chanakya's challenge, he got personal and heaped abuses on Chanakya. It was a clash of two uncompromising men, each unwilling to yield an inch of ground to the other, King Nanda also found Chanakya's manners wanting whereas Chanakya believed that Nanda was crossing the boundaries of professional conduct. Anger writ large on his face, Chanakya vowed that he would destroy the whole clan and tie his knot only after that. True to his oath, Chanakya ensured the end of the Nandas. Insulting Chanakya cost Nanda his kingdom and his life.

Today, you may have the upper hand. But it doesn't take long for the advantage to shift. Good times don't last forever. Treat others well and it will come back to you with interest.

6

Ego and Attitude

'Relationships never die a natural death. They are murdered by ego, attitude and ignorance.'

—*Buddha*

Once upon a time, there lived a Zen master.[4] People from far and wide came to seek advice from the enlightened soul. One day, a man of abundant wealth, who lived a luxurious life, visited him. He was not used to taking orders and had an air of authority. The master welcomed him and offered him a seat. He started pouring tea into a cup, ostensibly meant for the visitor. As the man watched in disbelief, the cup overflowed and the master did not attempt to stop.

'What are you doing, master? Don't you see the cup is full!' shouted the man.

The master laughed and said, 'Your mind is similar to the teacup. It is so full that there is no place for anything new to be added to it.'

The rich man's ego was coming in the way of acquiring knowledge.

To learn newer things, we need to have an open mind. Only then can we be receptive to knowledge. Learning is an endless process and knowledge is

[4] This story is inspired by Zen stories from Japan.

unfathomable. Most of us harbour the belief that we know everything there is to know, and what we know is enough. Nothing is further from the truth. Knowledge is akin to an evolving target. The moment we think we have gained as much knowledge of a particular subject as it is possible to get, something new is discovered and the target, which seemed so close, again moves further away from us.

Power and pelf are transient. As the ego starts consuming the person from within, pushing him further down the abyss, there is very little left of him in the days to come.

My friend and I were once discussing, among other things, about the ego of certain people. In a jocular vein, he asked me if I knew the expansion of ego.

When I replied in the negative, he laughed and came up with a gem. According to him, ego, when expanded, means 'everything goes out.' What he said made a lot of sense to me. Ego has various definitions and acquires different meanings as seen from the prism of philosophy and psychoanalysis.

Ego starts with 'I' instead of 'we', and 'my' as against 'ours'. Egoists live in their illusory world, far removed from reality. In their limited thinking, they are a cut above the rest and ahead of the pack. They do not want to be a part of the crowd and like to be treated differently. Individuals try to win arguments by using their position and authority instead of reason. Like leaders with less confidence in their own abilities who surround themselves with sycophants praising them all the time, egoists have a fan club that feeds their ego. Anybody who disagrees with them is promptly shown the door. They don't believe in respecting others' opinions or listening to contrarian views. In a way, they are trapped in a make-believe world. The fact of the matter is that your ego does not represent the real you. It is an artificial and superficial outer shell to cover your shortcomings. When the mask falls off, the hollow nature of the egoist is there for everybody to see. Ego is a kind of slow poison that takes over a person's character gradually and ultimately consumes them. As opposed to the ego, attitude has two facets—positive and negative. A person with a positive attitude is always ready to try new things, approaches and strategies; while those with the negative approach think that the best days are behind them and don't even try. Ego is an indicator of how you feel about yourself while attitude is how you physically manifest these thoughts and feelings.

Ego is akin to a virus trying to get into your system and is often the result of changed circumstances. When success goes to the head, it metamorphoses into ego. The achiever does not want to be seen with his colleagues and friends who couldn't come up in life and taste the kind of success he enjoys. For the person with an inflated ego, hc is in a different league altogether, oblivious of the humble beginnings from where he started. What he does not realise is that relationships are beyond positions and achievements.

While one might think that a big ego is a common trait among the upwardly mobile or the go-getters, the truth is that an outsized ego is anything but conducive to success; in many cases, it is counterproductive.

When we refer to a person with a king-sized ego, s/he lives in an ivory tower and expects their friends and subordinates to pamper and lionise them. The people surrounding such egoists might do so under duress and might be laughing at them behind their backs. This is nothing but a distorted sense of self-importance which gradually alienates them from the very persons they are dependent upon for professional success. Their relationships suffer and soon they realise that the people around are not offering the kind of cooperation such egoists have been used to. If they think that ego is one way of being confident, it is at best an illusion. While being confident is certainly good for most of the time, ego-driven individuals are often led by an extra dose of unhealthy overconfidence, convinced they are right all the time regardless of the facts.

But perhaps the bigger issue is that egoists in the corporate world are far too often seeking glory for themselves: 'Me before the company. Me before anyone else. I did this. I was responsible. It was during my tenure that...'

This is the kind of person who is obsessed with seeking glory, wants to get noticed and grabs credit at the drop of a hat. The upshot of this self-seeking attitude results in the focus getting shifted from company to self. Ideally, it should have been the other way around.

The problem of an inflated ego is a recognised one in the business world and has been the subject of many studies and debates over the years. While it is difficult to measure by any standards, attempts have been made to quantify the actual cost of egos in the workplace. A survey some years ago involving a sample of businesspeople in the USA found that the majority believed that those with bigger egos are responsible for poorer financial performance and affect anywhere between 6–15 per cent of annual revenue and thereabouts.[5]

Be it competition or business, egoists tend to underestimate the opposition. One of the first lessons in international sports is to never underestimate the opponents. At the world cup football championship held in Moscow in 2018, unheralded Croatia made it to the finals.

As we progress in life, quite a few of us taste success. With that comes confidence and self-belief which allows us to raise the bar and aim at seemingly unachievable goals. One thing leads to another and soon, you find yourself in a different league altogether, standing apart from the crowd. For those who have their feet firmly planted to the ground, their journey continues much to the envy of others. However, the flip side of success is ego which can water down the string of successes in a matter of minutes; the fact exemplified by this story.

Once upon a time, there was a scientist who was seized with the idea of cloning himself. He lost count of days he spent pursuing his single-minded quest, and eventually, years rolled by as he pursued his objective. Hard work and dedication always pay, and it was no different for our scientist. Ultimately, he succeeded in making a

[5] Virtugroup chairman Neil Petch on www.entrepreneur.com

replica of himself and it was well-nigh impossible to tell the original from the copy. However, the angel of death was not happy as the scientist was tinkering with the natural process of life and death. The shrewd scientist got to know that the angel was looking for him and created a dozen replicas of himself. The angel was confused as she looked at the 13 similar-looking men. Unable to recognise the scientist she returned, her mission unaccomplished. The scientist was elated as he thought he had tricked the angel and avoided death.

Nevertheless, the angel of death, who had a clear understanding of human life, did not relent and came back. She again approached the clones and commended the scientist for his extraordinary work.

She told the scientist that he was one of a kind and congratulated him on his stupendous accomplishment. However, she was quick to add that there was a noticeable flaw in his creation. That remark touched a raw nerve. His ego bruised, the scientist could not hold himself back.

'Impossible! What small flaw? You must be out of your mind!'

That was the giveaway the angel was waiting for and thus having identified the original scientist, carried him away. This is a simple lesson that even your skills can't help you if you don't keep your ego under control.

Committing and sticking to deadlines is more an art than a science, especially when you have acquired a new client. Before you commit, make sure you have the resources to deliver on time.

Now and then, you come across a few brilliant people who are authorities on their subject; have few takers as their ego and attitude become barriers to their progress. They do not listen to the advice of friends, well-wishers and colleagues and find themselves in all sorts of knots.

A former chief minister of one of the southern states of India wanted to build a new capital for his state, along the lines of Chandigarh. He was given an option to operate from Hyderabad, the future joint capital of the two states, for 10 years. He rejected the offer citing exclusivity and privacy. The outlay for the new capital was close to a billion $. He brooked no interference and had his way. His fixation for high-end technology, sprawling campuses, landscaping et al led him to misplaced priorities. Expert after expert advised him against shifting to the new capital as the move entailed huge investments. He was counselled several times against such mega projects. The experts felt that the same amount could be invested in hydroelectric projects, health and sanitation. Moreover, the state had to depend on the centre for funds, which was a variable factor. The chief minister thought otherwise and in his eternal wisdom, chose to build the new capital. As on date, the ambiguous project is hanging in the balance as funds have dried up. Further compounding the matter, he went hammer and tongs at the centre for not providing funds and walked out of the coalition. The coup de grace was delivered when his party was decimated at the hustings the following year. He lost everything—name, fame, power, position, status, goodwill, friends and was virtually staring at political irrelevance. The fall has been so precipitous that it might take years for him to be back in the reckoning. The wise electorate punished him for his ego which didn't contribute either to the state or the people.

Change is the only constant. Rigidity and obstinacy are roadblocks to attitudinal changes and leaves you far behind even as the world marches on. A positive attitude helps you adjust to situations and brings out the elasticity in you. The purple patch that you have been hitting consistently may soon disappear and you are facing an invincible adversary—destiny. It is here that your attitude will in all probability get you out of jail.

Not long ago, rightsizing was not uncommon in IT circles—employees were laid off keeping in view the top line and bottom line.

'We don't need you any more' was the line parroted ad nauseam.

I remember it was the year around 2017. The Indian IT industry, a behemoth clocking revenues of over 150 billion $, was facing rough weather. With a workforce of four million, they had every reason to smile, but not anymore. With the H1B visa crisis looming large, coupled with automation, the beleaguered industry was facing a double whammy. The country's top IT companies had been complaining for a while about the difficulty of picking up new clients. Automation, robotics and innovative technologies such as cloud computing were in great demand. The big three (Infosys, Wipro and TCS) along with a clutch of other companies were planning to lay off around 50,000 employees.

I was a mentor for young professionals. Amongst my mentees was Maya. She was working as an application development programmer in Bengaluru. Unfortunately, she was caught in the downsizing exercise undertaken by her company and lost her job. I put her through to a few of my contacts. As she left, I noticed a steely resolve, a never-say-die attitude in her.

I met her after a long hiatus and she was back on terra firma having secured a job with a start-up. Rewinding to tough times, she told me that she would leave home early morning and return in the evening. All the while, her parents thought that she was attending office, as she went from one recruitment agency to another armed with her biodata. With the perpetual smile on her face, the mask was well and truly concealing the turbulence within.

'Why did you keep your joblessness a secret?' I asked.

'No point sharing my sob stories as they have tons of their own,' she replied.

Sages in the days of the yore were unaffected by good or bad, success or failure, happiness or sorrow, life or death. In the modern world, emotional intelligence and empathy help you to be well grounded. Business is ephemeral but relationships are eternal. If your pride is bigger than your heart and your ego is bigger than your head, you will be a loner all your life.

In the epic Ramayana, the two antagonists Ram and Ravan have contrasting profiles. The latter is flamboyant while the former, a perfect gentleman. Ravan had mastered 64 types of knowledge, from the skills of Kshatriyas to the holy books of the Brahmins, which made him one of the greatest living asurs with wisdom and knowledge. He was an accomplished musician who played the veena with effortless ease. Though he was an embodiment of many good qualities and skills, a single frailty in character was enough to drag Ravan down. It was his ego that made him bite the dust.

7

Adaptability: The Key to Success

> 'What belong to you today belonged to someone else yesterday and will be someone else's tomorrow. Change is the law of the universe.'
>
> —*Bhagavad Gita*

A career in technology involves a fair amount of travel and on one occasion I had to visit Dubai, a fascinating destination and a major tourist attraction in the Middle East where the sand dunes, the gold souk and the Burj Khalifa beckon the visitor. After business for the day was concluded, my colleagues from my previous organisation working in Dubai would make it a point to show me the sights and sounds of the city. One such stop was the City Center Deira, a sprawling mall with the usual glitz and glamour. As I moved through the sections, I noticed many young boys and girls manning the counters. They were immaculately dressed and had a lot of poise and confidence. Most of them were from Kerala, the southernmost state of India.

I couldn't help noticing that they were interacting with visitors from across the world with the ease of professionals. I observed their communication skills and body language, all of which was always accompanied by smiles. The way they spoke English took me by surprise. Bereft of any regional influence, they went about their business as usual. In India, you can tell a person by his accent and virtually zero in on his state and location. But that was not the case here! How did this transformation happen? The answer lies in adaptability.

Adaptability is the key to success and survival. An individual who is ready to accept changes, sees an opportunity in the disruptive environment around her/him and thrives on it. Left with no choice, they need to adapt quickly to the environment; in such situations, rigidity is anathema.

Adaptability is hailed as one of the top skills in the fast-paced digital world of today where technology is changing by the hour. Companies are more interested in hiring candidates who are flexible, open to new ideas, recalibrate strategies and find solutions to intractable problems in the time frame available. Every professional wants to climb the corporate ladder in the shortest possible time. As s/he changes jobs, s/he notices that the cultures vary across companies and organisations. In a career spanning over two decades, I have had the good fortune of working across a range of environments. As a young engineer, I joined a government-run company, which was the nation's top public sector engaged in deep-sea drilling for oil and gas.

The work culture was akin to any government organisation with project delays, ownership issues and accountability.

After 10 long years, I switched over to another company down south in Bangalore, India, which was in the automotive space with its head office in Germany. The German headquarters had a different culture. It was heavily invested in technology and any change in the systems was affected after getting the approval from the headquarters. The processes were methodical and centrally controlled.

I worked for nearly two years when an excellent offer came my way. It was a quantum leap where I was given a position in the senior management level of a company which was into stocks, shares and electronic trading and based in Mumbai. Though the company was floated by the cash-rich financial institutions of India, the work culture was different—not intrusive, with a lot of freedom and emphasis on quicker execution and delivery.

After spending six years there, I joined an IT company which was into business consulting and outsourcing. A majority of the clients were based in the USA. The company had modelled their processes to suit their clients. Midnight conference calls stretching to the early hours of the morning, reviews and progress meetings were perfectly normal, given the time difference between the USA and India.

Though it took me some time to get adjusted, I soon found out that it was not as tough as I had imagined. In a matter of months, I was comfortable.

Inflexible individuals live in the past and oppose change. They prefer to continue being in their comfort zone for as long as possible without considering the changes that keep occurring in the larger world, ones that could even affect their jobs. Adaptability is the ability of an individual, team or organisation to adjust or change to best meet the needs of the situation or environment. In the event of a change, a flexible person and his team will adjust to the newer set of circumstances and figure out a way to optimise their performance in the new situation rather than oppose it. Adaptability begins by getting integrated into the company culture, embracing new technologies and respecting their processes. Until and unless you are one among them, you are the odd man out in an otherwise cohesive work environment, often sticking out as a sore thumb. Inflexibility is the bane of all human beings and the desire to change and adapt has to come from within, both at a mental and physical level.

The two soft skills that will help you adapt to circumstances are emotional intelligence and a positive attitude. Instead of viewing the new job with scepticism and constantly drawing comparisons with the previous one, look forward to it as a new learning experience, one that will contribute immensely to the reservoir of knowledge you already possess.

Emotional intelligence helps you bond with the new team. This leads to easier adaptability when working with new teams and helps develop a better rapport with colleagues.

> *Adaptable people not only adjust to change but accept it.*

They accept change, hone strategies for dealing with the unknown and shift their behaviour to accommodate new situations and challenges.

Adaptability is not limited to human beings but extends to animals, birds, reptiles and the elements as well. On land, for example, the Siberian tiger is at home in the wild, where temperatures swing between -35°C to 5°C. Whether it is big cats or desert reptiles living in the scorching heat of 50°C, they have all evolved over the years and adapted to the changing environments. Take the case of the sidewinder, a snake found in the desert areas of the south-western USA and north-western Mexico. As ground temperatures soar during the day, the snake keeps a portion of its body above the surface of the sand to ward off heat.

During the dry season, water is scarce. In the monsoon season, the rainwater fills up lakes and ponds. In due course, the monsoon clouds move away and water becomes scarce again. As the levels recede, fish find it difficult to breathe. But the African lungfish has a trick up its sleeve; it covers its body with a secretion, goes into suspended animation without food and water and wakes up after two years as the first drops of rain bring relief to the parched landscape—a state of samadhi.[6]

For humans, these are all lessons in adaptability. In the business world, cultures, processes and philosophies vary across companies, regions and verticals. Orientation programmes help employees get acclimatised to the new set-up. The quicker they adapt the better it is, as a more important task is at hand—to perform and deliver in the new surroundings.

[6] A yogic stage, at which union with the divine is reached before death.

Adaptability is a skill that has no bounds. It is in great demand for the simple reason that technology, processes and environments are changing by the minute. The sooner you embrace these changes the better, else you become irrelevant in what is fast becoming a volatile, uncertain, complex and ambiguous (VUCA) world.

So, how does one develop adaptability skills?

Be ready for change that can occur at any moment. Do not have an emotional attachment to your area of work, whose expiry date has long gone.

Read what is current and see how it can add value to the project you are working on. Prior preparation is a must when one is faced with change or changing over into a new job, rather than walking straight into it.

This reminds me of an unforgettable experience I had several years ago when I visited the Sri Ramana Maharshi ashram in Tiruvannamalai in Tamil Nadu. Far removed from the high-stress business world, I spent two days in the serene environs where peace reigned supreme.

The earthiness and simplicity of the place attracted devotees in droves. Away from the material world of gadgets and gizmos, many foreigners seeking spiritual rejuvenation would spend a few months here before going back. I noticed that men had changed into shirts and dhotis with the vermilion tikka on the forehead. The ladies wore simple cotton saris with prayer beads around their necks. All the inhabitants of the ashram would go about their daily routine in much the same way as others.

At lunchtime, I saw them partake of the spartan food with no complaints. Coming from some of the most advanced countries in the world, they were at ease, sitting on the floor and eating from a plantain leaf with bare hands.

I have heard a lot about adaptability. Here, I was seeing it in action. I was curious as to the reason they had left the comfort of their homes and come here. I soon got my answer: They had come in search of peace and they were prepared to change to find it.

Adaptable people flourish amidst chaos while the rigid fumble. Success is both a journey and a destination. Those who adapt, find solutions to problems by getting out of their comfort zone because they know that the answer lies beyond its limits. If you are courting success, flexibility is the key.

A mid-sized company with a workforce of 500 was using the Microsoft mailing system. The users were pretty comfortable with the simple and plain Outlook. One fine day, the company was taken over by a transnational group that was wedded to the IBM culture. In a matter of days, the Microsoft mail was replaced by Lotus Notes—a mail application native to IBM. The employees, left with little time to react and adjust, were curtly told to switch over. The result? People left the company in droves!

Why did they leave? It is not that they hated IBM and its proprietary culture. They weren't diehard Microsoft fans either. They needed time to change and the bolt from the blue unsettled them.

Change management is a process which ensures that transition happens smoothly with minimal disruption. Ideally, the company should have informed its associates months in advances of the impending changes, which they failed to do. By taking them into confidence and training them on the new mail system, the surprise element would have been addressed.

Adaptability is not just about change; it's also about how we change ourselves to fit into the ambience or the new environment. This is easier said than done. Adaptability is an admixture of confidence, self-belief and creativity. Not everybody is gifted with these qualities. Leadership is all about seeing the change and acting accordingly.

History is replete with stories of companies which were leagues ahead of the competition in terms of market share and were lulled into thinking that the halcyon days would last forever. What followed was a meltdown with the exalted position of such companies irretrievably lost.

In the early 1990s, Nokia introduced its flagship product, the 2110. The mobile phone was flying off the shelves. Twenty million pieces were sold and in the next three years, Nokia's had the lion's share of the international market. Closer home in India it was well above 60 per cent and rising.[7]

In 2008, Google released an open Android operating system (OS) where the emphasis shifted to mobile applications. This resulted in the development of hundreds and thousands of apps, ready to be deployed on mobile phones. Apple too joined the fray. Nokia didn't see the change coming as they were in an illusory comfort zone.

[7] https://www.fortuneindia.com/enterprise/nokia-the-revenant/103573

The result was that the android became a rage and Nokia's market share plummeted from 39 per cent (2009) to 5 per cent (2012).[8] It was Google and Apple all the way, reducing Nokia's home-grown Symbian OS to a relic of a bygone era.

The above example is a combination of smart and not-so-smart leadership. What should have Nokia done? The answer is simple. Along with the native Symbian, they should have joined hands with Google and simultaneously developed the Android OS. The market forces would have guided them on the need to junk Symbian and move towards the more open Android OS.

They didn't change at the right time and thus, unfortunately, bit the dust.

How do we improve our adaptability? Where do we start? While it is a natural skill, adaptability can be developed and mastered as well. Here are some tips to help improve this skill.

Observe and monitor changes in your environment: You will not see the need for a change until you notice changes in your environment. Adaptability must be timely. Always make a conscious effort to monitor trends, values, attitudes, etc. Compare present observations with past ones and find out what has changed. For instance, a low customer-retention rate despite an increased sales figure is an indication that disgruntled old customers need attention.

Be willing to learn: Observation alone is not enough. If the result of your observations suggests, you need to

[8] https://www.zdnet.com/article/nokia-reinvented-decline-resurrection-and-how-ceos-get-trapped/

learn something new, do not hesitate to do so. While you can learn some things on your own when furnished with appropriate educational resources, others may require tutorials from specialists. Don't decline to use the services of a professional tutor if necessary.

Avoid procrastination: Don't just be willing to learn. Take the necessary course of action. Remember that adapting oneself is more effective when the change occurs; preparing yourself for the change is even better. For instance, your competitors started diversifying after the industry faced a decline leading to an inevitable collapse. However, you started a new trade after the old industry had collapsed totally. While you are still a novice with a very small customer base, your competitors might build a wider network of customers and suppliers in the new industries.

Acknowledge the fact that changes are bound to occur. We are living in a world where obsolescence has to be accepted. The technology of yesterday may not yield a solution to the problem of today. A new thinking and a new approach will stand you in good stead in the disruptive world that we all live. But one can look at disruption as an opportunity rather than a threat. In uncertain times, the onus is upon us to deliver and do a good job at that.

> *It is not the strongest or the most intelligent who will survive but those who can best manage change.*
>
> — *Charles Darwin*

8

Relationships

‘Business is ephemeral, relationships are eternal.’

On quite a few occasions in the past, I have come across people with short memories; rather, they chose not to remember. As the head of IT of a company, evaluating proposals, interacting with equipment supplies and system integrators, price negotiations, placing orders was part of the job. Right from telecom equipment, computers, cabling and networks, suppliers for all kinds of equipment would visit my office.

Years after I left the corporate world, I tried to establish contact with them. None of them bothered to respond. In their limited thinking, they assumed that I was seeking business. I always try to revive a lost contact, not with the intention of doing business but to recall the past when we worked together. Call it nostalgia, but I have always experienced a sense of joy when I meet people after many years. The clock rolls back as those wonderful memories of bygone days come alive. You are transported back in time.

In today’s material world, every call or meeting is seen through a monetary prism. What’s in it for me? Money doesn’t last forever. Relationships do, minus pecuniary benefits and commercial angles.

The unforgettable lesson you learn about relationships is—never foreclose. In life, every relationship contributes to our growth in some way or the other; especially those you have written off thinking that you will never meet them again. Keep them open-ended as long as possible as that person you meet might be a game changer. In these current uncertain times, foreclosing a relationship is not a good idea, as this real-life incident reveals. More often than not, you come across the same person with whom you were not on the best of terms. It's a small world and what better way to drive home the point than a real-life incident.

Raj was a person with a mind of his own. He had a couple of run-ins with the present boss with whom he had worked for four years. Many derisive comments and snide remarks later, he couldn't take it any longer and decided to move out. As the courier boy rang the doorbell, Raj knew that it was the offer letter from the company where he had applied for a position. After putting his papers, he had to complete one more formality—the exit interview. This was his chance to get even with his boss. He had nothing to lose as he was leaving the company for good. At the exit interview, emotions got the better of him and he unleashed a fusillade of insults using intemperate language.

Raj joined the new company with dreams of a better work environment and a more reasonable boss. A week into the job, Raj realised that the job wasn't as cushy as it seemed. He saw red everywhere. The new boss made him work till 11 PM. Weekly reviews and rebukes left Raj incapacitated. Two months into it made him uncomfortable and he realised his mistake. He decided to go back to his old company and sought an appointment with the boss from his previous place of work. Pensive and unsure, he entered the office of his erstwhile employer and was greeted by his former colleagues. He was made to wait the whole day, at the end of which he was told that the boss was too busy to meet him and there was no guarantee that the meeting would take place. The acrimonious loop was well and truly closed, this time by his old boss.

The corporate world is not a Bollywood film where the hero mouths a fiery dialogue and walks away in a blaze of glory. Burning bridges is not the solution. Keeping the doors open is. Skirmishes and engagements are a part of boardroom meetings and should be forgotten over tea and biscuits. At work, nothing is personal. Conjuring utopian images of the new assignment is not uncommon. Relationships assume importance in the volatile and uncertain world of today. More often than not, you will run into the same person you were averse to working with. In business, there are no permanent enemies or friends and it might not be a good idea to terminate a relationship in the heat of the moment. The grass is not always greener on the other side.

Relationships are not based on wealth, position or status. Friendship is pure and sublime, beyond the materialistic world. There is a certain innocence you find in schoolchildren who share lunch from their tiffin boxes. As they grow up and go their different ways, they seldom recognise each other.

The story of Krishna and Sudhama should serve as a reminder for all those who value friendship. As children, both study under Guru Sandipani in the gurukul. Sudhama is the son of a poor Brahmin but that does not come in the way of his forming a strong friendship with Krishna. After completing their education, they go their separate ways. Krishna becomes the king of Dwarka and lives in a palace. Sudhama, steeped in poverty with a family to support, finds it difficult to make ends meet.

One day, he decides to seek help from Krishna and travels to Dwarka. On seeing Sudhama, a teary-eyed Krishna rushes to embrace him. Once inside the palace, Sudhama is treated like a king. Krishna personally washes his feet and offers him food served on a plate made of gold. Sudhama is overwhelmed. He is in two minds about going through with his decision to ask Krishna for help. After careful introspection, he decides against it and prepares to return.

'My friend. What gift have you brought for me?' asks Krishna.

Sudhama unwraps a piece of old cloth and gives Krishna a handful of dry rice flakes. Krishna accepts the offering and tells his friend that the flakes are very tasty. Unknown to Sudhama, Krishna blesses him with riches. Sudhama thanks Krishna and leaves the palace. As he reaches home, he is surprised to find that his humble dwelling is transformed into a palatial house with all the riches. His wife is very happy and Sudhama's difficult days come to an end.

In my experience, I have seen people cultivate relationships with a motive. If a representative from a big business house is visiting the office, the staff goes out of the way to make him comfortable. There is, of course, nothing wrong in treating a potential customer with courtesy and care but it should be across the board, without discrimination. We must realise that relationships, especially in business environments, are not built in a day. It takes months and years for the reliability factor to set in. Much depends on your service. Quality and time are the two clinching factors that determine the longevity of a relationship. Transparency and honesty are the other.

Meet the relationship managers of a different kind! Nobody has taught the small shop owners not backed by MBA degrees nor have they been exposed to the kind of education we have received. Yet, they master these skills on their own and become successful. I visit a medical shop regularly. On one such occasion, I purchased medicines worth a few thousand ₹ and gave the chemist my card to swipe. Though there was enough balance, the connection was not being established. I told him that I will pick up the medicines the following day. He politely gave me the box of medicines and told me to make the payment at my convenience. This is a fine example of relationship-building based on trust. No wonder the chemist is popular and many people in the locality speak highly of him.

Fast-food joints are sprouting everywhere like mushrooms. Apart from multiplexes, food lovers throng to restaurants to have a meal or snack of their choice. The two parameters that determine the choice of the restaurant are quality of food and prompt service. Both may or may not be available at the same place. Customers pick their eating places according to their priorities. Some are fastidious about taste and won't mind travelling distances and waiting in queue to dig into their favourite dish. For others, time is at a premium and they look for quick service while willing to compromise on taste.

You place an order and sit there salivating at the prospect of digging into your favourite dish. Half an hour later, the dish is served. The taste is out of the world but the delay has upset you. As against this, the other restaurant is known to serve customers on time. In less than five minutes, your dish has arrived. You marvel at the efficiency, not before discovering that something is amiss. It doesn't taste as good as the one where the dish was served to you after a long wait. Each restaurant is building a relationship with the customer based on one of the parameters described above. While the first scores on taste, the second more than makes up for quality and taste by serving on time. Customers will patronise the eating houses based on their priorities. We are unconsciously building relationships in every kind of interaction, from home to office, office to market and market to home based on our needs, our priorities and those which suit us best.

Family relationships have a bearing on everything else. Next comes the office, where careers are made and it is in our interests to build as many relationships as possible. Holding on to past grudges manifests in the form in negative energy and in no way will contribute to your success. This is easier said than done, but it is important to remember that there is no place for emotions at the workplace. Everything is official. People who abuse or use harsh language at the office don't have the answers to your questions.

If we look at sports, the players however resentful and aggressive on the field, in the course of a match, shake hands at the end of the game. The same holds good in the corporate world where differences should be laid to rest at the end of the day.

The world is small. It is possible that many years later, you might meet the same person in a different setting to discuss a business deal. Never write off relationships. If you bury the hatchet, they might even recommend you to another company. Let the parting be polite and not acrimonious so that you can get past the friction and conflict.

Leaving a company with a bitter taste in your mouth will reduce your business prospects, especially if the other person has quickly scaled up the corporate ladder and is in a position to decide things.

Keeping in touch with your old colleagues helps you get business leads. Remember, you don't have to talk about yourself and your accomplishments all over again. A good portion of it will be done by your former colleague.

When you leave a company for better prospects, you bid farewell to your colleagues. What most of us tend to overlook is that they will also look out for greener pastures and follow suit. As you go up the ladder in your career, so do they. In the small corporate world that we live, it is quite possible that you will run into each other at some event or seminar. While recalling those good old times you spent together, it also leaves the window open to further opportunities. The advantages of keeping in touch can never be underestimated.

A bit of a personal touch in a professional association leaves a lasting impression. When I left my old company after serving for many years, a colleague threw a farewell dinner party in my honour—a gesture I could never forget. Ten years later, we got in touch through social media and stayed in touch. He even helped me, by personally closing a training programme with a prospect by putting in a good word.

Helping your friends in difficult times shows your human side. Life is based on reciprocity. You need to help your connections in difficult times too, a gesture which is bound to yield dividends in the long run. Keep building contacts and keep your network alive. Sometimes, the law of averages works and you start hearing from unexpected quarters.

I found writing a good way to build relationships. I write regularly and have been successful in building a base of followers who read and respond to my stories and posts. Somewhere, your posts should touch the lives of readers and make a difference to their lives. That, according to me, is the beginning of a relationship.

A few years ago, competition was the buzzword and companies would go to any length to win a contract, including bad mouthing and showing the competitor in a poor light. Over the years, competition lost much of its sheen and it was time to go beyond the shibboleths. On the digital highway, collaboration pushed competition to the background. What is the reason behind the paradigm shift?

When you are competing, the one thing that is foremost in your mind is to win at any cost. You have to beat the opponent and you channelise a lot of energy into achieving the win. The irony is that you have to go through the same exercise again and again, which will tire you out in the long run.

Collaboration, on the other hand, has the potential to build relationships for a lifetime. There are no winners or losers. You are on the same side. The whole is greater than the sum of its parts. Another reason why collaboration trumps competition is the fact that with the former, you combine diverse skills and expertise, which opens a bigger market to explore.

Collaboration also brings out your generous side where you believe in sharing your success with others. Once personal bonds are established, you cultivate a friendship that can last for life.

The first lesson in building a lasting relationship is to not expect anything from it. Just as a plant doesn't grow overnight as soon as you sow the seed, one can't reap the benefits of a relationship in the shortest possible time. Initially, both parties are circumspect. Trust needs to be built. Over a period of time, both parties are presented with opportunities to prove their loyalty and support. It is here that the wheat gets separated from the chaff. True relationships withstand the test of time. Mutual respect and a helping hand in times of need takes the relationship a few notches up.

Events and seminars are great places to meet several like-minded people and start new relationships. While mail, telephone conversations and video calls are good for a start, there is no substitute for meeting in person. Verbal and non-verbal communication, together with voice modulation and emotional intelligence, plays a vital role in making a success out of a relationship.

In the average human lifespan of about 70 years that is at our disposal, we must go all out to build relationships. You don't have to wait for the other person. Make the first move and at every conceivable opportunity, introduce yourself to people, customers, contacts and in the process, build a rapport. These are the seeds, you have sown today, that will eventually grow into a tree and yield fruits tomorrow.

Finally, I will leave you with a story which more than epitomises the shades of emotions at the opposite ends of the spectrum. I distinctly remember the unforgiving winter of Bengaluru. It was the month of December in the year 2017. On a cloudy Wednesday, I hired a cab to go to a meeting. With the traffic at its peak at the time, the driver decided to take a shorter route which cut through a posh residential area.

'Do you see the small window of that house, sir?' he asked me.

'Yes, I do. What is so special about it?' I responded.

'Last week, I left an old couple at the door next to the window. Both are in their 70s. They spent a lot of money and educated their son. After graduation, he went to the USA and worked for about 10 years. Then he returned and got married to a girl who developed a pathological dislike towards his parents. The couple was blessed with a son and the grandparents' joy knew no bounds. The child was more attached to them than his parents. Five years later, the man decided to move out, leaving the old couple to fend for themselves. The child was missing his grandparents. To this day sir, the grandparents visit the house but are not allowed inside. Their visitation rights are limited to 15 minutes of conversation with their grandson through that window before it is slammed shut.

Five minutes of viewing time is all that they get in return for bringing up their son, educating him and sending him to the USA so that he would have a head-start in life. As they bid goodbye to the child at the end of the allotted time, the boy cries uncontrollably till he is pulled back. I witness this drama every week sir.'

It takes years to build a relationship and a few seconds to destroy it.

9

Against All Odds!

'As soon as the fear approaches, attack and destroy it.'

— *Chanakya*

If there were no failures, who would have thought about success! A world full of joy would have led to a unidimensional existence. There is no black without white; it is only where there is darkness can there be light. Every question has an answer and every problem, a solution. Life throws up myriad challenges at you. Do you have the gumption to take them head-on?

In August 2017, I was travelling in an autorickshaw in Bengaluru, the city where I live. As I got in at the back, I noticed an unusual extension at the rear of the body of the three-wheeler. For a moment, I thought it was a new design. Curiosity got the better of me and I asked the driver the reason for the unusual protrusion at the back of the vehicle.

'Sir, my baby is sleeping at the back.'

When I turned back, I could see the toddler, hardly a year old, blissfully asleep and oblivious to the harsh realities her dad was facing.

'I am 32 years old and have been driving this auto for the last five years. My wife used to look after me and my two children. She was a pillar of support, right from caring for our children to attending to my old parents.

Unfortunately, she died from a mysterious illness leaving me to care for our children. My son, the elder of the two, is studying in class two. The little girl you see at the back is my daughter and I carry her with me for the first half of the day. My parents look after her for the rest of the afternoon.'

As he finished his story, I could hardly believe what I had seen and heard. How cruel could life be? We see many heroes and heroines on the silver screen but here I was seeing one in real life. His grit, determination and above all, the courage to face life despite this harsh reality was a lesson for all of us, who keep cribbing for every little thing. It reminds me of the tale of a barefooted man complaining about not having any shoes until he saw another without a leg.

Just like the tsunami, mishaps don't give you prior notice. Today it may have befallen someone else, but tomorrow, it might just be you. Adversities, ranging from losing a job or a loved one, financial losses or unexpected health problems, will upset the balance that you believe you have achieved in your life. It's tough to see the light at the end of the tunnel when it seems that all odds are stacked against you. I have been through similar circumstances and have experienced that sinking feeling that threatens to drown you in depression. It is that mixture of despair and helplessness which reduces you to a hapless spectator as destiny dons the mantle of the wrecker-in-chief.

Whenever I am faced with trying times in my life, I have always taken recourse to philosophy to calm the nerves.

More often, you are not the only person who is at the receiving end. Out there in the big bad world, there are many who suffer similar fates and would have been written off. A few summers later, they bounce back disproving all calculations. They are back in the reckoning in the blink of an eye, much to the surprise of their detractors and critics.

How do they do it? When the wind is blowing against you, there is no point trying to escape or outrun it. Cataclysmic changes will upset the apple cart but no cyclone lasts forever. At the outset, the problem looks huge and unsolvable. Break the problem into small, manageable pieces and engage with them one at a time. The human mind and body is not conditioned to multitask for the simple reason that you cannot go to the second task until you finish the first. Multitasking is nothing but fast-paced 'single' tasking.

The greatest glory in living lies not in never falling, but in rising every time we fall.

However, there is a downside to multitasking. In our hurry and excitement to complete too many tasks, we end up completing a few but fail to nail the rest of them. This brings us to prioritisation. If you complete the first two jobs on your list, you may not finish the rest of the tasks. But that should not be the cause for worry. Call it failure or whatever you would like to, there are quite a few learnings that help you to deal with the unfinished tasks. Treat it as an opportunity to test your skills and consign to oblivion, all negative thoughts. Revisit your strategies and try a different approach. In 300 BCE, Chanakya had an axe to grind with the Nanda kings who had insulted him when he went to them seeking employment. Along with Chandragupta Maurya, he attacked Magadh but the numerically superior Nandas easily defeated the forces of Chanakya and Chandragupta. The duo barely escaped with their lives and decided to sketch out another plan of action. One night, as Chanakya was returning home, he overheard a mother scolding her son who was having his dinner. On the plate was a mound of rice with hot dal[9] in the middle. The boy accidentally put his hand in the dal and burnt his fingers. On seeing the child writhing in pain, the mother admonished the boy.

'Don't start eating from the middle of the rice heap. It is hot in the centre and you will burn your fingers like Chandragupta did. Start eating from sides.'

These words opened Chanakya's eyes and it became clear to him that they needed to devise a better strategy to attain victory. He realised his mistake of taking the enemy head-on and thus prepared to attack Magadh from the fringes. Chanakya along with Chandragupta left Magadh and travelled to the outskirts of the Nanda kingdom. They raised an army and started capturing the regions of Nanda kingdom from outside while moving towards the core (Magadh) with each win. They made huge gains and overran territories. With each success, their popularity kept rising and by the time they reached Magadh, the citizens were in awe of the young Chandragupta. They welcomed him with open arms, eventually leading to Dhana Nanda's defeat.[10]

[9] Dal - dried,split pulses.

[10] Sastry, Rudramurty. 2011. *Chanakya* (Kannada). Bengaluru: IBH Prakashana.

Many a time, things do not go as per plan. Nearly two years ago, I had submitted a training proposal to an organisation based in the United Arab Emirates (UAE). I had spent months customising the business communications programme to meet the exacting standards set by them. They were pretty satisfied and probable dates and travel plans were discussed on the phone. I was excited and was looking forward to the trip. The wait seemed eternal. Finally, they got back to me saying that the programme was put on hold.

Closer home and around the same time, another client from the technology sector informed me that the five-day soft-skills training programme covering accent training for their call centre executives had been put on hold indefinitely. Lightning never strikes twice, they say; but here I was, hit repeatedly by bolts of rejection, wondering if I was the sole exception to the quote. It was the beginning of a dull phase, a period of inactivity and frustration.

Countering a dull phase is like challenging the elements. Throwing in the towel was the last thing on my mind. Much like the lungfish which hibernates for months, I put my soft-skills training activities in a state of suspended animation and concentrated on an area I was familiar with—music.

Many years ago, I had trained in the Hindustani and Carnatic genres of Indian classical music. I had honed my skills as a singer as well. Music is a much sought-after subject and I hit upon an idea to translate it into a language understandable to the layperson. I combined my writing and training skills to drive home the concept of ragas,[11] the origin of music, singing, modulation, beats, keyboard notations and emotions to an audience keen on knowing the basics. I took this concept of a musical workshop to a few music clubs in Bengaluru and the response was quite encouraging. Since then, I have been holding musical workshops regularly. As a speaker, I have had the pleasure of answering questions on various aspects of music. Professionals from the corporate world have shown interest in a half-day session on how music helps in self-development, how one can be a better human being through music and how music can boost performance levels at the office.

A group of doctors were keen on exploring the effects of music on patients. It is also believed that certain ragas help cure illnesses and the curative properties of music is a subject of animated discussion in many clinics around the world. As I continued to enjoy this phase as a musicologist, I was aware of the fact that very soon, I would have to go back to my true calling.

Dull phases, characterised by periods of inactivity, may be turned to our advantage if we fall back on some of our skills or hobbies. They stand you in good stead and can see you navigate through difficult phases.

I am also a firm believer in the law of averages. Good and bad times are cyclic—neither lasts forever. Dull phases are a blessing in disguise as they provide the much-needed respite to recharge your batteries before getting back into action.

You often wonder why you didn't succeed where people with less talent have made it. That was

[11] A combination of different notes in Indian classical music.

probably because they did not look at a lack of talent as a hindrance to success; they did not consider it a limitation and broke free from their comfort zone. They grappled with situations they had never encountered before and worked on their skills and talents. They were prepared to take the rough with the smooth, often at the risk of being at the receiving end of mockery. They were thick-skinned and focused enough to take any kind of humiliation and insults thrown in their way in their stride because they knew that the fruits of labour would just not be a game changer but a life changer. Leaving the comfort zone puts you in touch with your abilities, lying dormant for years in search of a challenge.

Life is unpredictable, more so in the technology world. You have the job one day and it's gone the next. In the uncertain times, we are living in, it is always good to think that your job is on the line; the axe may fall anytime. More often than not, it has nothing to do with your performance. Extraneous factors over which you have little or no control are responsible.

There is no point digging a well when the house has already caught fire. One of the strategies that people follow is to always apply for a job irrespective of being employed or not. The only indeterminate factor is time. It is very rare to find a job waiting for you the moment you quit. Another approach is to set up a parallel activity the moment you take up your job. I have seen many professionals take to writing, teaching and counselling. Though not a monetary substitute for a well-paid job, it will put you into an active zone where you will get a platform to display your skills.

History is full of stories of about succeeding against all odds. Valmiki's Ramayana is a treatise on people who triumphed through sheer will and determination. Ram, the seventh avatar of Lord Vishnu, faced hardships throughout his life. Though born into a royal family, he was forced into exile for 14 long years. He had to leave the palace and spend his time along with his wife Sita and Lakshman in the forest. His problems didn't end there. In their absence, Sita was kidnapped by Ravan and held prisoner in Lanka. With the odds stacked against him, Ram continued his search for Sita. After meeting Hanuman and forging an alliance with the Vanar Sena, he marched to Ravan's Lanka but another challenge awaited him—crossing the vast ocean that separated Ravan's kingdom from them. With the help of his allies, he built a bridge over the ocean. Ram finally accomplished what was a seemingly impossible task—of triumphing over a fierce and formidable adversary like Ravan and rescuing his beloved wife from his clutches. His story should offer each of us enough inspiration to overcome obstacles and never give up till the end is achieved. The human incarnation of Vishnu had to fight his battles just like an ordinary mortal and yet he emerged victorious.

10

The Ethics of Business

'It takes 20 years to build a reputation and five minutes to ruin it. If you think about that, you'll do things differently.'

—*Warren Buffet*

In the early 1990s, a multinational conglomerate invited offers from companies for a megaproject. The response was overwhelming. After going through the proposals, they shortlisted six companies—three Indian and three Japanese. They were asked to make individual presentations and the Indians were invited first. The presentation, replete with data and PowerPoint slides, impressed the panel. Each company was told that they had competition from the two other companies from their own country as well. On being asked their opinion about the others, the Indian companies tried their best to run down the other companies. Stories of client dissatisfaction, plummeting profits and incomplete projects sprouted up from nowhere to reiterate that business with the other two was a risky proposition. All three companies stuck to the same narrative when asked about each other. Now it was the turn of the Japanese companies to make their presentations. They too were asked their opinion about their compatriot companies. To the surprise of the panel members, representing the multinational conglomerate, each of the participants spoke highly of the other two. They told them that their competitors were as capable as anyone else to execute the project under discussion. No attempt was made to show the other two in poor light. What happened was beyond imagination. The project was divided into three phases and all the three Japanese companies were awarded a phase each. Asking them about their competitors was the proverbial red herring. Capabilities aside, the panel was probing the participants for their business ethics.

The origin of the concept of business ethics can be traced back to the 1960s. Today, with growing competition, every company tries its best to project itself as an entity built on the constructs of honesty and transparency. Business ethics have developed into standards of moral and ethical responsibility the world over.

When I introspect about business ethics, I usually ask myself the question—why do you need to be dishonest or cheat the company you are working for? Should you decide to do so, is it not the case of biting the hand that feeds you? You have a good job with an equally good pay packet. The company has bestowed faith in you. You have been given unrestricted authority to negotiate the big-ticket items. I think that if you have your basic needs covered and live a comfortable life, then excess money is superfluous and doesn't help you in any way except landing you in trouble. The question that we need to ask ourselves is, how do those huge amounts of money earned through unscrupulous means make a difference to your life. Life is otherwise smooth sailing.

Do not throw a stone in an otherwise placid lake and create unnecessary disturbance.

Why should you upset the apple cart for no reason at all? What is surprising is that in a moment of weakness, very senior executives, who should ideally be setting an example for the younger generation, make one false move before going down the precipice, never to rise again.

Other than unfair practices by professionals while being a part of the company, another reason why the image of a business entity gets besmirched is due to the inability to say 'no'. You are under pressure to meet your targets. Providentially, you come across a business prospect who is interested in a long-term association with you. It is a juicy offer, too tempting to refuse. But the fact of the matter is that you don't have the resources to commit to the time frames and deadlines set by the client. Caught between the desire to take on the project and an awareness that you simply won't be able to meet their deadlines, your mind starts working overtime. You end up committing to an unrealistic deadline, knowing fully well that there is a strong possibility that you won't be able to meet it. As months roll by, the client sees through the game and pulls out of the contract. Your competitors grab the opportunity with both hands while committing genuine time frames. Word is out in the market that you have lost a lucrative deal. To make matters worse, the client is pleased with the competition, with whom they sign a three-year contract.

The reason for this mishap is an unethical approach, which you start by committing to a deadline you knew was unachievable. But, what could you have done to save the situation? If it were me, I would have discussed the details of the project threadbare with the client, making them fully aware of my resources and limitations. I would have apprised them of what I could deliver under the given circumstances. In the worst-case scenario, they wouldn't have agreed as the time frames were not compatible, but the upside to that was that the client would have left with a positive image of me. That would have left me in contention for future projects.

It is not enough to just do business; it needs to be done the right way. Business ethics are not edicts etched out in stone but a set of unwritten rules. It is assumed that honesty and integrity are inalienable traits, deeply ingrained in human beings. Every company has policies enshrined in the rule book. It is against company policy to accept illegal gratification or indulge in corporate espionage. Showing the company in poor light in public fora or dressing inappropriately at work go against standard norms. On its part, the company you work for is duty-bound to support you through thick and thin. Besides a good salary, it offers certain benefits like insurance, healthcare, child education and stock options. In short, the company takes care of your family as well. It has reposed faith in you and, in turn, expects you to contribute to its growth. In a scenario like this, why would you rock the boat?

The lure of money drives people towards unethical business practices. Crossing the line puts the employee to high risk. You may not see eye to eye with the boss or the management but that would not justify resorting to any sort of impropriety. Your philosophy and work ethic may clash with that of the company. The better option for you is to quit than remain in a system where unethical practices are encouraged.

Back in the 1990s, Nick Leeson, a British trader in his twenties, was hired by Barings, a UK bank, based in Singapore. The maverick trader was hailed as the next big thing and was known for his daredevilry in placing trades. Initially, he made good profits, pushing up the market capitalisation of the bank by as much as 10 per cent. However, in subsequent trades, he lost close to 208 million pounds and unscrupulously, hid the losses. To recover them, he placed a short straddle on the Nikkei which went the other way, bringing down the oldest British merchant bank. Cancer caught up with Leeson while he was in jail. After serving for four years in a Singapore jail, he was released on compassionate grounds. And to think that when he first started with the bank, Leeson was earning £12,000 a year annually and would have lived like a king.

Nine years later and good 2,000 miles away, a similar drama was unfolding in the city of Hyderabad in south India. Described as a scam of epic proportions, one of the top four IT companies was caught manipulating accounts to the tune of 1.5 billion $. On the verge of collapse, the company was bailed out by the Mahindra group. The chairman and a few members of the top management spent over four years in jail on charges of falsification and embezzlement. As a former employee of the company, I was saddened at the turn of events. A monolith almost bit the dust before it was rescued.

There is nothing wrong with earning money or courting the privileges of power and pelf. Overlooking the ethics of business will only result in short-term gains. A meteoric rise is a temporary illusion. Once your reputation is sullied, no amount of money can ever get it back. Socially ostracised and condemned to a life of obscurity, one would go so far as to think that the jail is a better place to live. As Sir Walter Scott fittingly penned, 'To the vile dust from whence he sprung, unwept, unhonoured and unsung.'[12]

While few cases might mar the otherwise unblemished corporate landscape, some companies swear by business ethics and will go to any extent to abide by them. Transparency and honesty are concomitant in all dealings, irrespective of the ticket size. In the early 2000s, the Tatas came up with massive investments in Tamil Nadu. Right from basic telecom services, internet, data centre and cloud-based apps, they were all set to build a world-class digital infrastructure in Chennai and establish a beachhead in the south. The planned investment ran into billions of ₹. As the company started digging for laying a network of fibre-optic cables, the ruling dispensation picked up the scent and their eyes fell on the loot.

Their efforts to stop the digging fell through as the Tatas, known for following the rule book right down to the last word, held their ground. The lawmakers didn't stop at that. An emissary in spotless white appeared at their office and hinted at percentages. The regional head explained to him that he wasn't the right man to talk to and put them on to the senior management at Mumbai.

[12] The line is from Sir Walter Scott's poem 'The Lay of the Last Minstrel', Canto VI, 'Breathes There the Man'.

The senior management replied that it was against the rules of the company to get into such transactions. 'In that case, you will not be allowed to resume work' was the terse one-liner from the powers to be. Later, they relented as word got around that the Tatas were pulling out of Tamil Nadu and going elsewhere with their investment. In the words of Ratan Tata: 'I ferociously wanted to ensure that my successor has total commitment for ethics and values, we fought for years now.'[13]

I didn't have to go very far as the managing director of the company where I was working was indulging in unfair practices. He was anything but honest and looked at every opportunity to make money at an age when people turn philosophical and think of the greater good of society.

I was looking at techno-commercial proposals for the purchase of computer systems from a host of vendors. It was a big-ticket item and he wanted to favour a particular company. I showed him the compliance statement and proved to him that the company didn't stand a chance. Moreover, the commercial bid was on the higher side and the value proposition was not convincing.

'You change the figures. Nothing will happen.'

This came as a shock. I politely told him that it is against work ethics and it wouldn't be possible for me to do it. He held it against me and denied me a promotion even though I had worked for nearly six years in the same position.

[13] Ratan Tata said this in 2010 when a Tata Motors factory had moved from Singur to Gujarat.

Many years after I left the company, I saw his photo in the papers where he was led away to jail as an ordinary criminal on charges of embezzlement. The long arm of the law will catch up with you in the long run.

Transparency and being above board are qualities one should possess by default. It takes a person of great character to stand their ground and say no to inducements. In a moment of weakness, the best cave in, only to repent later.

Honesty and integrity may not make you rich or, for that matter, even successful! But you are assured of a good night's sleep at the end of the day.

In 2002, the United States Congress passed the Sarbanes–Oxley Act (SOA) to address accounting and corporate scandals and to develop a code of ethics for senior financial officers. The act also requires corporations to have a code of ethics that promotes honest and ethical conduct, full disclosure and compliance with governmental regulations. Somewhat similar to the SOA is Clause 49 of the Securities and Exchange Board of India (SEBI) regulations. It was added to introduce some basic corporate governance practices in Indian companies and brought in a number of key changes in governance and disclosures (many of which we take for granted today). It specified the minimum number of independent directors required on the board of a company. The setting up of an audit committee, and a shareholders' grievance committee among others, were made mandatory as were the Management's Discussion and Analysis (MD&A) section and the report on corporate governance in the annual report, and disclosures of fees paid to non-executive directors. A limit was placed on the number of committees that a director could serve on.

Unethical behaviour has serious consequences for both individuals and organisations. At the individual level, people can lose their jobs and reputations while this behaviour occurring at the level of the company can lead to them losing their credibility, causing a decline in general morale and productivity, as well as significant fines and financial losses. Professionals who lose their jobs as a result of unethical behaviour are not considered for similar positions in other companies. The stigma of corruption is difficult to shake off as nobody wants a tainted executive in their ranks.

It is one thing leaving a company due to differences with the management and totally another to be jettisoned out for unfair practices. Apart from the workplace, the individual's social life is also affected as s/he prefers to avoid parties, events and conferences. This also has a bearing on the family and children as there is a high chance of them being socially ostracised. Worse still, criminal cases attract jail terms, adding a new dimension to the suffering and mental torture the person is going through.

You will realise the value of freedom when you go to jail.

There is no difference between ethics in business and ethics elsewhere. You have been honest as a student. You have come up the hard way in life. You are respected as an icon in the industry circles. People quote you in their speeches. It has taken years for you to establish yourself as a consummate professional. You have been recognised by your company for your valuable contribution. You have been promoted for your body of work. You have contributed significantly to the growth of the company.

Somewhere, the lure of money will force you to take a wrong step. Are you going to succumb? Run the risk of letting your reputation, which you have built assiduously over the years, dissolve like salt in water? If you do let avarice get the better of you, you will inevitably have to pay a price. When you do, the edifice crumbles and you are not the person you were a few years ago. All your efforts and sacrifices get watered down. Friends, close acquaintances and well-wishers are nowhere to be seen. You belong to the living dead. As long as you follow ethics in business and elsewhere, scandal can never touch you and there are high chances that you will find contentment in your life.

11

Take the Initiative

'Initiative is doing the right thing without being told.'

— *Victor Hugo*

In the days of the yore, a village was struck by torrential rains that led to floods, causing the house to be submerged. A man trying to escape the deluge ran towards a tree and began climbing. The water level started to rise alarmingly. The young man was cornered and ultimately consumed by nature's fury.

When he reached the pearly gates, he confronted the angel, 'Why did you let me die so soon? I was in the morning of my life and you didn't raise a hand to help me!'

'Not once but thrice I tried to help you,' said the angel. 'A man sitting on a higher branch of the very tree you were climbing asked you to move up. You ignored him. The second time I sent a boatman who shouted at you to jump into his boat. But you were afraid to do so and let the opportunity go. Finally, a log of wood floated by, very close to the tree. All you needed to do was to cling on to it and remain afloat. I help those who help themselves and sadly, you were not in that category.'

They say opportunity seldom knocks twice at your door. Few realise the importance of seizing the moment while others let them pass to repent later. Going back to the days of Partition, there was a lot of bad blood between India and Pakistan. Four wars and numerous cross-border engagements did very little to assuage bitter feelings on either side. Back in 2001, the Agra Summit is remembered as one of the greatest missed opportunities of India–Pakistan relations. Former Pakistani foreign minister Khurshid Mahmud Kasuri in his book, *Neither a Hawk Nor a Dove*, wrote that the 'solution to Kashmir was in the grasp of both governments'. Then Pakistani president Pervez Musharraf had proposed what was called the Four-Point Solution to Kashmir. According to different accounts, the solution was, in principle, acceptable to Prime Minister Atal Bihari Vajpayee but the deal fell just hours before the signing ceremony.

Life is an equal opportunity-employer and creates a level playing field for go-getters to succeed. The rest miss the bus.

In the same way that water finds its level, people have to find or create work for themselves. When we talk of initiative, we look at people who find their way through the maze. No hand-holding is necessary. They start from scratch and are emotionally attached to their work. Right from defining the problem and going through every minute detail, they work with passion and equanimity for they know the enormity of the exercise that lies in front of them.

Initiative is a quality you find in self-starters. According to a Chinese proverb, 'The man who removes a mountain begins by carrying away small stones.'

Confidence, patience and creativity are the tools employed by men and women who take the initiative in several ways. In any project, everything is hazy in the initial stages and the path becomes clear as you cross one milestone after another. While others doubt your abilities, only you know that there is a treasure trove of talent within you which has to be unearthed sooner or later.

Long ago, there ruled a hard-working king who ruled over lazy subjects. Since the kingdom was prospering, they found no cause to work as they enjoyed all the comforts that life had to offer. They never thought beyond their own selfish needs and wouldn't participate in anything to do with community service and socially responsible work, such as keeping their neighbourhood clean or planting trees. One day, they were surprised to find a ditch on the main road covered with a boulder. It was right in the middle, obstructing traffic and inconveniencing people. Some avoided the obstacle by going to the left of the ditch while a few others went to the right. The athletic jumped over the ditch while quite a few took a different route altogether. The next day, the king summoned his subjects and asked his guards to remove the stone. Underneath was a chest full of gold and silver coins. In full view of the contrite populace, the chest was moved back to the royal treasury.

'If any of you had moved the stone, the treasure would have been yours,' said the king.

There are quite a few takeaways from the story. Go-getters unearth hidden opportunities. For those who are complacent, opportunities are lost by staying far too long in the comfort zone.

Many years ago, I happened to read a book written by Burke Hedges titled *The Parable of the Pipeline.*

The book mentions two ambitious young men Pablo and Bruno, who wanted to make it big in life. The residents of the village depended on a lake for water. The lake was far away. Pablo and Bruno sensed an opportunity and manually started transporting buckets of water to the village. For every bucket, they earned a $. While burly Bruno carried larger buckets and earned money faster, Pablo had other plans.

He realigned his goals and started digging a channel. Displaying tenacity and grit, he completed the arduous task in two years and earned while he slept and ate. Pablo didn't exchange time for money. Instead, he built a pipeline for a cushy life ahead.

Meanwhile, the wear and tear on Bruno's body was all too visible. With advancing age and earnings down to a trickle, he couldn't go on any longer.

In today's high-pressure environment, there has been a paradigm shift in the way people work. Working smarter ensures you achieve your goal faster, rather than spending hours toiling away. In Hedges' book, Pablo, the pipeline-builder, certainly thought out of the box and grabbed the opportunity even when the whole village laughed at his idea.

From individual initiatives, let's now zoom out and consider this from a much larger perspective. When countries are involved, taking initiative pays rich dividends. With the Cold War well and truly forgotten, collaboration is the new mantra that is bringing nations together. Today, bilateral relationships between nations are based on trade and technology rather than one-upmanship and brownie points. While I don't hold a brief for any political party, it must be appreciated that the present dispensation took several initiatives to build strong and robust relationships with countries across the world. From the USA to Europe, South East Asia to the Middle East and from Central Asia to Africa, India enjoys a position of pre-eminence. These initiatives have brought huge amounts of foreign direct investments. Despite the COVID-19 pandemic, the country is poised to bounce back and well on its way to becoming a preferred investment destination and one of the vibrant economies in the years to come. All this despite the mayhem caused by COVID-19; it is hoped that a vaccine is just around the corner.

Initiative and creativity move the world. They foster the realisation of innovative ideas in various industries and contribute to constant development. There is a great demand for energetic professionals who are inventive and enterprising enough to be proactive in everything they do.

While we take initiatives in everyday life, it is all the more important to take similar initiatives at the workplace. Who doesn't want to rapidly scale the corporate ladder? There are two kinds of professionals who occupy the corporate space—the reactive and the proactive. While the former acts in response to a situation, the latter is well in control and ready for any exigency. The proactive professional gets singled out for appreciation as s/he is the person who goes the extra mile. If you wait for instructions from the boss for every little step, you will wait forever. Spoon-feeding is passé and associates who can work independently and produce results rule the roost.

Let us look at the advantages of taking the initiative at work. Personally, the individual gains a lot in terms of knowledge and skill and learns more about the company and the market it serves. He is exposed to new challenges and won't be stuck in the same old routine. Initiative entails seeing something that needs to be done and either doing it or figuring out ways to get it done.

Spotting people who take the initiative, according to me, is a fairly straightforward procedure. When a team leader announces that there is an opportunity to work on a new project and asks who is interested, not all hands go up. Those who put up their hands show passion, interest and zeal to work on the new project. People who take on the responsibility are the same people who will take the initiative. This also reflects leadership qualities, as leaders never hesitate to take up challenges. The window of opportunity is limited and shows up for a finite period, which is why such moments have to be seized. Professionals with initiative grab it at the right moment and transform it into a success.

If you are taking the initiative to work on a sizable project, it is important to build a healthy and harmonious relationship with your team members. The days of the one-man show are over and team support contributes to making the project successful. In an official environment, taking any kind of initiative is an agglomeration of a slew of soft skills. A well-grounded professional has in their arsenal a good mix of soft skills—adaptability, emotional intelligence and empathy.

Social interactions are drivers for team building. This does not have to do with propagating big celebrations—small gestures work well to promote camaraderie and help build cohesive teams.

I rewind to my Tokyo days. I had few friends but Hinata was an exception. Thanks to his stay in the UK for many years, he spoke good English and doubled up as my man Friday too. He would come in very handy as a translator for information on hotels, trains and cab fares.

One day, he invited me to his office, a small outfit of 30 people. I reached an hour before the end of the day and I seemed to be just in time to observe a daily practice followed by the office associates.

All the employees would assemble 15 minutes before closing time and have tea and biscuits together in a spirit of bonhomie and friendship. Hinata told me that this practice was being followed for years and the bonding helped them function as a coherent team.

I had a very valuable takeaway from observing the above example: Not every experience is pleasant in our day-to-day life. Some are negative and trigger an emotional response from within, which is quite natural. What is worrisome is that you carry it for days, weeks and even months. As time passes, the excess baggage becomes heavier by the day, till it can reach a point where it gradually wears you down, not allowing you to concentrate on the job at hand. Like a person possessed by a spirit, negative thoughts hold sway. Revenge and retribution are foremost in your mind. We need to purge these thoughts as soon as possible and make space for positivity.

Positive thoughts will take you places—that was the message that was conveyed subtly at Hinata's office.

Let me share an initiative that I took to start a company called TLRNOW, which was founded by a group of three professionals who met on the LinkedIn platform and had worked in the corporate space for the better part of their lives. The company is mainly into training, coaching and mentoring. The services are available both online and onsite. The courses range from leadership, communication and time management to yoga, health and image consulting. These courses are offered by experts who have a distinguished track record in their areas of specialisation. As I was surfing the internet, I came across a TEDx programme which set me thinking: Can just one talk show to cater to the needs of 1.3 billion people? I saw a lot of space for quality talks across topics and domains. Knowledge and information cannot be the exclusive preserve of metros. In a country with a broad landscape, the two- and three-tier cities are not far behind, what with a record number of start-ups mushrooming in these little-known towns and cities. After considerable introspection, I firmed up the strategy and set things rolling. I discussed the idea with my team and we were all on the same page. The time had come to take the initiative and launch a talk series which would be closer to the Indian psyche.

This is how TLRTALKS was born. In today's changing world, mere domain knowledge is not going to guarantee success. To prepare the students to face the challenges at the workplace, our talks and seminars cover topics like leadership, communication skills, time management, handling stress, public speaking, presentation skills, behavioural changes, relationship building, voice modulation, accent and campus-to-corporate programmes. The talks are delivered by seasoned professionals who understand the pulse of the industry. The attendees benefit by listening to some of the top professionals in the industry covering a whole range of topics. Staying current is what is important today and these talks focus on some of the latest trends in the industry in technology, life skills, disruptive thinking and mentoring, thus aiming to help accelerate career growth.

With 'Lifelines' as its tag line, TLRTALKS, a not-for-profit initiative, is just not a forum to express oneself but a knowledge dissemination hub, a space to find answers from experts to nagging questions through real-life experiences and a chance to stay ahead of the ever-changing digital landscape.

While it is still in its early days, the year-old TLRTALKS has conducted over 25 programmes covering many two- and three-tier cities in India. We have plans to launch many more TLRTALKS across the nation. Due to the pandemic, we are planning to hold these talks in the second quarter of 2021. It is an idea, an opportunity, we didn't want to pass for we knew that this initiative is bound to make a difference to people's lives.

Take the initiative without breaking your head over the outcome. No road is strewn with flowers for you to walk on. From a king to a common man, the ride will inevitably be bumpy. Better it is to take the initiative and enjoy the journey as you watch the sapling grow into a tree.

12

The Comfort Zone

'Life begins at the end of the comfort zone.'

Once upon a time, there lived a king who was respected by his subjects. He had a passion for game hunting and would often go the forest in search of quarry. One day, he received a gift of two magnificent falcons and his joy knew no bounds. He summoned the royal falconer and instructed him to train the birds. Weeks passed and one day the royal falconer sought an audience with the king. He told him that of the two, one falcon was flying majestically, soaring high in the sky, while the other bird had not moved from its branch since the day it had arrived.

The king summoned healers, magicians and sorcerers from across the kingdom to tend to the falcon and promised them a hundred gold coins. Unfortunately, none could make the lazy raptor fly. He decided to fall back on his courtiers and assigned the task to them. Even that move didn't get the desired result. The next day, when the king looked through the palace window, he noticed that the falcon had still not moved from its branch. Having tried everything else, the king thought to himself, 'Maybe I need someone more familiar with the countryside to understand the nature of this problem. Go, get somebody from the countryside and ensure that he makes the bird fly.'

The king's soldiers spread themselves across the kingdom and met many people including peasants, farmers and tillers. As they were interacting with people, a farmer ventured forth and told them that he would solve their problem. The soldiers laughed at him but ultimately decided to give the farmer a chance. The farmer travelled with the soldiers and was shown the bird. The farmer asked for a saw and got down to work. He finished his job within an hour and left as quietly as he had come without even bothering about the reward.

In the morning, the king was thrilled to see the falcon soaring high above the palace gardens. He said to his court, 'Bring me the doer of this miracle. I would like to reward him suitably.'

The guards went back to the farmer and told him that the king was keen on meeting him. The very next day, he was made to appear before the king. As he stood silently, the king asked him, 'How did you make the falcon fly?'

With his head bowed, the farmer said, 'It was very easy, Your Highness. I simply cut the branch on which the bird was sitting with a saw'

It is clear from the story that the reticent bird soared to new heights after being forced out of its comfort zone. Seemingly alluring, the comfort zone is a space where you wish to stay forever. The boat is steady as you wade downstream with little or no effort. But, is there a flip side to it?

The comfort zone is a state of mind where a person is in control of factors which otherwise would have induced stress and heightened levels of anxiety. The fear of the unknown doesn't exist in the comfort zone. Here, performance levels are steady. You are enveloped by a false sense of security. Getting out of the comfort zone is not easy. Horses rested during weekdays also need to be coaxed out for the Saturday derby unlike those who are in the habit of a daily canter irrespective of whether there is a race or not.

Before going to the other side—the discomfort zone—let's try to find out why people prefer to be in the comfort zone. The zone offers you safety. Things have worked for you in the past and will continue that way. Why upset the apple cart? Camps on either side have good reason to defend the zone of their choice. Not everybody is willing to get out and soil their clothes. In due course, they realise that the comfort zone has no variety. It is dull and monotonous where nothing ever changes. All the action, excitement and thrills are outside this zone and they yearn to be a part of it. The uncharted terrain has much more to offer than the cosy confines of the comfort zone. It is beyond this zone where they can move from mediocrity to excellence and obscurity to fame.

Right from my college days, I was interested in music and started singing at small events and functions. Everybody praised me and told me that I was destined to be the next big thing in the music industry. I was thrilled to bits and conjured up visions of performing on the big stage. Then, pursuing a career put a stop to these aspirations. Many years later, I wanted to pick up from where I had left off to pursue my hobby. I was advised by many to get trained in classical music, which

I thought would be a good place to resume my hobby; so I went to a guru. On the first day, he asked me to sing a few notes and I was struggling. My world came crumbling down like a house of cards. The session revealed the gap between an amateur and a professional. I was struggling to reach the higher notes. The story was no different with the lower octave. Subsequent sessions revealed the limitations of my ability as my vocal cords for years had operated within the confines of the comfort zone and their capability had been untested over the years.

Slowly, I began understanding the basics of the ragas, taal[14] and my singing range. My problem was far from over as another challenge was staring me in the face. For a classical singer, an accompaniment like the harmonium or a keyboard is a must as it helps them set the starting note, leading into delineations and exploring the depth of the ragas. I had never touched a keyboard in my life and had to start from scratch. Though I had worked on the keyboard on a laptop, the musical keyboard was an entirely different cup of tea. Right from memorising the notes, playing the keys in sync with the beats while singing proved quite a handful. It took me a couple of years to get the hang of it and understand the science behind playing the keyboard. My fingers would ache and at times, I harboured ideas of giving it up. I knew that the keyboard was not my comfort zone and I had to put in some extra effort to master the technique.

We don't realise this but it is the discomfort zone that we should be in. The name is a misnomer and on the

[14] Rhythm or beat

face of it, may even seem discouraging and avoidable. But this is where we really get to explore our abilities and potential, and even find out our limitations—as well as ways to overcome them

The comfort zone is a transit lounge and it's difficult to stay there forever. Should you decide to leave its perimeter and venture outside, a certain amount of physical and mental preparation will stand you in good stead. Out there in the discomfort zone, the terrain is rough. Confidence, patience and self-belief are the only qualifications you need.

The comfort–discomfort zone crossing is a veritable Maasai Mara—an uncharted wilder land if you will—where many factors are arrayed against you. You will only be able to stand up to them if you are made of sterner stuff. Over a period of time, after you do conquer the obstacles, this discomfort zone becomes the comfort zone and it is time to leave.

The discomfort zone teases and taunts you, often challenging your limits. This is bound to lead you to frustration and desperation. The only solution to the problem is baptism by fire. Though exhausting and incapacitating, that is the only way to separate the wheat from the chaff. The tough survive the rigours of the journey while others fall by the wayside. Do you have it in you to cross the line? Only time will tell.

Ironically, the much-despised discomfort zone holds the key to your success. The technological progress that we have made in areas of science, agriculture and technology bear testimony to the fact that man has repeatedly tried to come out of the comfort zone and succeeded to a great extent. In this case, the grass is greener on the other side. Confidence, perseverance, self-belief and patience are the mantras that will help you cross new frontiers.

A lunar space probe fires a series of booster rockets to escape earth's gravitational pull. Similarly, you need to summon all your strength and courage to leave the zone. And that is just the beginning because on crossing over, it isn't as though success is waiting to greet you with open arms. The real struggle begins now. The first set of people who cross the zone are risk-taking individuals. They wish to change the quality of their lives. They are keen to bring their hidden and undiscovered talents to the fore. They are aware of their potential and look to break new ground. A little success here and they are on their way exploring newer horizons that never existed before. It is a vindication of their self-belief and sets the platform to harness their potential to the fullest. They are not a part of the crowd anymore. Parking in the comfort zone gets you nowhere.

Hedges, in his bestseller, *The Parable of the Pipeline*, asks: 'Would you be a bucket carrier all your life or build a pipeline for ongoing residual income?'

Life begins at the end of your comfort zone. A mother took her schoolgoing son to the doctor for a regular eye check-up. As the boy was put through various tests by the optometrist, the mother was relaxing in the clinic reading a paper. The boy's report was ready and the lady was called in.

'I hope everything is okay, Doctor?' she casually quipped.

'I am afraid that is not the case. Your son has no vision in his right eye.'

The lady felt the earth moving under her feet even as she tried to fight the sinking sensation that was creeping all over. She gathered herself and told the doctor that there was no family history of visual impairment. Both she and her husband had normal vision. Then the doctor calmly explained to her that the boy was suffering from the lazy-eye syndrome. In layman's language, the affected eye was not being used and the entire visual burden fell on the left eye. The right eye, in the absence of its normal function, had gone into hibernation. Since the boy was young, the line of treatment, besides eye drops, was to put a patch on the left eye and force the right eye to resume its normal function. On similar lines, you possess a range of skills which have been lying dormant and largely untested. These skills are in a state of suspended animation and are itching to come alive at the first opportunity. It is incumbent upon you to provide that opportunity by crossing into uncharted territory.

One of the reasons why people don't venture out of the comfort zone is the fear of failure. Persons who have a propensity to take risks and try something new break out of the rut and escape the monotony of a unidimensional existence. Those who accept failure as the first step to success are perfect candidates to leave the comfort zone. It is better to fail and learn from the experience than to stay in the comfort zone forever and get rusted in the process. People who constantly challenge themselves, set and accomplish new goals. In such people, every failure only strengthens the resolve to succeed. It is a stepping stone to success. Go-getters do not stay in the comfort zone for long.

But how do you come out of the comfort zone?

If you are a sulking individual, cursing your fate and doing nothing about it, it is time you introspect and set your life in order. Self-pity is the last stop before throwing in the towel. Break out of the home–office–home rigmarole. Try different things. Meet new people or perhaps try a new hobby—reading, storytelling or drama. New subjects, a new ambience and a new set of people with whom you have never interacted before will do wonders to your mind and heart. What are the benefits of coming out of the comfort zone? You can lead a full life and enjoy the experience. As you meet people and cultivate new contacts, you will open a few more doors. For all you know, opportunities might come knocking at your door. The introvert in you needs to be given a decent burial.

Many years ago, I used to write for some of the leading newspapers in India on topics ranging from technology to business. After a gap of many years, I thought of going back to my first love—writing. I was on LinkedIn for many years but in the role of a passive reader. I would have my afternoon siesta and go through many posts. A few years ago, I decided to come out of the comfort zone and write posts on business, technology, training, soft skills and almost every topic under the sun. Fortunately, my writing skills were intact and my number of followers increased. Even my mailbox, which had gone into sleep mode, became active as the responses to my posts were on the rise. The crowning glory was an offer to head a company engaged in training, coaching and mentoring. The offer from one of India's top publishing houses to bring out my book was the perfect icing on the cake. This is my first-hand experience of the advantages of leaving the comfort zone.

If you are still in the comfort zone, it's time you leave it.

13

Empathy

> ‘Empathy is often defined as understanding another person's experience by imagining oneself in that other person's situation: One understands the other person's experience as if it were being experienced by the self, but without the self actually...’
>
> —*Sara D. Hodges and Michael W. Myers*

The review meeting was going on, as it usually did. The long hours stretched endlessly. The chief executive officer (CEO) was sitting at the head of the table. The young workforce was a bundle of energy, well aware of the competition and the need to get things moving. On the surface, everybody looked relaxed; the undercurrent of seriousness was barely visible.

Suddenly, a female employee excused herself. When she didn't return, the CEO got up and found her waiting outside the board room. She was too dazed to speak. Having just received the news that her father had had a heart attack, she was in a state of shock.

The CEO went back into the board room, apprised the gathered team about the situation and aborted the review meeting. He went back to the shocked employee, reassured her and booked her a flight home that very afternoon so that she could be by her father's side as soon as possible.

He didn't just stop at that. He accompanied her to the airport and continued reassuring her of the support of the entire office. Late in the evening, he called her for an update on her father's health.

Beyond the veneer of corporate sophistry and one-upmanship that characterise businesses, every person has a humane side. Top and bottom lines aside, we cannot escape from problems and challenges that make us go through the gamut of emotions. Today it may have been someone else, but tomorrow, it might be you. Empathy for your colleagues and employees is what makes a great boss. While not all bosses are understanding, and the ones who are might be in the minority, empathetic bosses show their human side when a colleague or an employee is in distress.

The slot was vacant for far too long and the company was in a tearing hurry to recruit a candidate for a middle-management position. The HR head was given a week's deadline to fill the position.

The team went into overdrive. Six candidates were shortlisted and the interviews were spaced across three days with two candidates appearing in the forenoon and afternoon sessions each day. The first two days went without a hitch. On the third day, they had finished the morning session when they received a call from the last candidate. She was unable to make it due to an exigency. Enquiries revealed that the lady's eight-year-old son had recurring fever and she wasn't in a position to attend the interview.

The HR chief, in a spot of bother, summoned up courage to speak to the CEO. He convinced him to defer selection by a week, which was accepted grudgingly. The lady was given a chance to appear for the same interview a week later.

Whether the decision of the HR chief was right or wrong can be up for debate, but the fact remains that it was taken in the best interests of the company and the potential employee.

> *As you turn the pages of the rulebook, somewhere, unseen to the human eye, is a chapter titled 'Empathy', which only a few can read.*

Everybody is not equal. Where there is plenty, there is poverty. Hope and despair are two sides of the coin. Some are lucky and some are not. Empathy allows you to see others through their eyes. The ability to be empathetic will enrich you as a person and give you a well-rounded character. Empathy is a feeling, a skill that becomes a part of your system, not just at the office but in your approach to life.

After a hectic business meeting, the famished executive parked his car and made his way towards a roadside restaurant. He settled down at a table next to a window, from where he could get a clear view of the street.

The ravenously hungry man ordered a three-course meal as well as dessert. The dishes occupied the entire table as he dug into the delectable spread, oblivious of the surroundings. A few minutes into his lunch, he looked up and noticed a boy and a girl looking peering through the glass. One look at them and he knew that they had not eaten a good meal in days. He invited them to his table and ordered the same set of items for them. Their faces lit up with happiness as the children relished the pasta and the ice cream. As they sauntered out of the restaurant satisfied and delighted, the executive asked the waiter for the bill.

The waiter returned and presented the bill. The man was shocked to see that the restaurant hadn't charged him a penny for the food. Thinking that they had made a mistake, he went to the counter to pay the fare.

'Thank you, sir,' said the restaurant employee manning the counter. 'Humanity is not charged.'

It is one thing to be rich and successful but quite another to be human.

Humanity cuts across barriers of wealth, status and money. Not all are born alike and nature sometimes is unkind. While there are many able-bodied persons, there are people in the world who are specially abled. Kindness is not limited to human beings but should be extended to animals and birds as well.

A farmer was going through hard times and decided to sell his puppies. He painted a sign advertising the sale of the four pups and nailed it to a post on the edge of his yard. As he was driving the last nail into the post, he felt a tug on his overalls. He looked down and saw a little boy.

'Mister, I want to buy one of the puppies.'

'Son,' said the farmer, as he rubbed the sweat off the back of his neck, 'these puppies come from fine parents and will cost a good deal of money.'

The boy dropped his head for a moment. Then, reaching deep into his pocket, he pulled out a handful of change and held it up to the farmer.

'I've got thirty-nine cents. Is that enough to take a look?'

'Sure,' said the farmer. And with that, he let out a whistle.

Out from the kennel and down the ramp ran Dolly followed by four little balls of fur. The little boy pressed his face against the fence. His eyes lit up with delight. As the dogs made their way to the fence, the little boy noticed something else stirring just inside the doghouse. Slowly, another little ball appeared, this one noticeably smaller. Down the ramp it slid. Then, in a somewhat awkward manner, the tiny pup began hobbling toward the others, doing its best to catch up.

'I want that one,' the little boy said, pointing to the pup.

The farmer knelt at the boy's side and said, 'Son, do you really want to take that puppy? He will never be able to run and play with you like the other dogs.'

Hearing that, the little boy stepped back from the fence, reached down and began rolling up one leg of his trousers. In doing so, he revealed a steel brace running down both sides of his leg, attaching itself to a specially made shoe. Looking back up at the farmer, he said, 'You see, Sir, I don't run too well myself, and he will need someone who understands.'

With tears in his eyes, the farmer reached down, picked up the little pup and gave it the boy.

I could relate to the story more than anybody else. I was born with congenital cataract and as a child, I couldn't see anything beyond a few feet. In medical parlance, cataract is a condition in which the lens of the eye becomes progressively opaque, resulting in blurred vision. Those days, technology was not so advanced and the best that the doctors could do was to test my vision and recommend spectacles. When I went to school, my parents would request the teacher to allot a seat in the first row so that I could see the blackboard. Reading was a challenge as my eyes would turn watery ever so often. I would often wonder how others could see things from a distance so easily and would often search for answers. My parents did everything possible to find a solution but to no avail. Partial blindness was a challenge while writing exams too. For the board exams, I carried a magnifying glass as I could not see the barometer markings for the practical examination in physics. It was the same with the bachelor's degree in engineering, which were, in effect, five long years of struggle with partial eyesight.

My parents taught me a valuable lesson. Make the best use of your abilities under the circumstances. I wanted to become a doctor but my impaired vision forced me to become an engineer. At 37, I underwent a lens-implant procedure and for the first time in my life, I could see the world so bright and full of colour. I will never forget the dark days I have been through. In the words of Helen Keller, 'The best and most beautiful things in the world cannot be seen or even touched—they must be felt with heart.'

Today, when I see a blind man crossing the street, I rush to help. I know what blindness is. I have been through it and can empathise with people whose visual faculties have been snatched away by the cruel hand of destiny for no fault of theirs.

Psychologists Daniel Goleman and Paul Ekman[15] break down the concept of empathy into the following categories:

Cognitive empathy is the ability to understand how a person feels and what they might be thinking. Cognitive empathy makes us better communicators because it helps us relay information in a way that best reaches the other person. Surgeries were nothing new to me and I was wheeled into the operation theatre a couple of times in my life. Just after graduation, I was all set to board a train and take a job in city, thousands of miles from where we lived. That very night, I had severe pain in the stomach. The doctors told my father that it was a case of appendicitis and an emergency surgery was required. The operation had to be performed within 24 hours, failing which the appendix would burst. The surgeons not only did a good job but were a jovial lot, telling me that it was a fairly simple and straight forward surgery of a routine nature which they perform regularly. I was reassured that it was indeed necessary and I was ready to take on the world once it was over. When I came to my senses, they even showed me the appendix that was removed.

Let's take a case where your office colleague is facing surgery and is nervous. This is the first time he is undergoing surgery and has the butterflies-in-the-stomach feeling. Since you have gone through the cycle, you put yourself in his position and help him deal with the fear. You tell him that he is not the only person on

[15] Goleman, Daniel and Paul Ekman. 2009. *Knowing Our Emotions Improving Our World*. This audio book is a conversation between Goleman and Ekman.

the planet who feels that way. It is a natural feeling and any misgivings about the operation can be put to rest by talking to the doctors and nurses. You speak to him and drive home the point that he needs to be courageous and confident.

Subsequently, psychologist Sara Hodges and author and researcher Michael Myers noted that while empathetic people feel distressed when someone falls, they aren't in the same physical pain. This type of empathy is especially relevant when it comes to discussions of compassionate human behaviour. There is a positive correlation between feeling empathic and the willingness to help others.

'Many of the most noble examples of human behaviour, including aiding strangers and stigmatized people, are thought to have empathic roots,' according to Hodges and Myers.[16]

The other kind of empathy, compassionate empathy, goes beyond simply understanding others and sharing their feelings: it moves us to take action, to help however we can. It forces the individual to move from the theoretical to the practical plane. For instance, when a road accident occurs, and the victim is lying on the ground, a crowd gathers around the injured man who is bleeding. Though they feel for the person and discuss road accidents in great detail, nobody lifts a finger to help the victim as seconds tick away. It is worth mentioning an incident which brings alive the finer aspects of compassionate empathy. A few years ago, the Karnataka minister of health was going to his office in Bengaluru.

[16] Hodges, Sara and Michael Myers. 2007. 'Empathy'. In *Encyclopedia of Social Psychology*, edited by Roy F. Baumeister & Kathleen D. Vohs.

As his car neared a junction, there was a commotion on the street, where a motorcyclist had fallen. The minister immediately put the man into his car, drove to the nearest hospital and informed the staff to give the man the best possible care. He also left instructions with his staff to check and report the status of the man by the evening. Once he was convinced that everything was under control, he drove back to his office.

The third kind of empathy, emotional empathy, is the ability to share the feelings of another person. Some have described it as 'your pain in my heart'. This type of empathy helps you build emotional connections with others.

In life, we come across many people who are going through tough times. They may come to you asking for help with a lot of hope. Do not shut the door on their face. Empathise with them. Recall those days when you were running from pillar to post in search of a job when perhaps a good Samaritan with tons and tons of empathy turned out to be your saviour. He went above and beyond, even speaking to his contacts and followed up with them. He didn't rest till you received your appointment order. To this day, you are indebted to him. Now it is your turn to return the favour to a different person. They say it is better to give than receive. Empathise with the needy and bring back the smile on their faces so that they can look at a happier tomorrow.

To help is your karma. To receive is his.

14

The Art of Negotiations

> 'Let's never negotiate out of fear.
> But let us never fear to negotiate.'
>
> —*John F. Kennedy*

Life is full of negotiations. You will not get what you deserve until you negotiate. Negotiation, an offshoot of the exfoliating communication tree, is an integral part of business and is at a confluence of a variety of skills, from articulation, empathy and domain knowledge to flexibility. Negotiation skills are just not limited to business and finance and fall under two broad categories—the formal and the non-formal. While the former deals with day-to-day interactions, the latter has a more serious flavour, manifesting itself in salary negotiations, legal contracts, sale, purchase and service-level agreements. Your negotiations begin from the moment you step out of the house, go on through the day right till you reach home after a hard day's work. You would have negotiated with the cab driver, the vegetable vendor, the fruit seller and the laundryman. As you haggle for a better deal, the one thing that is on your mind is value for money. A penny saved is a penny earned. Irrespective of the type of negotiations, what is common to both formal and non-formal negotiations are principles.

Some time ago, I was privy to an argument between a lady and a vegetable vendor. The lady descended on the scene in a mid-sized luxury car and approached the vendor who had spread the vegetables on a mat. She started haggling with the poor man over a mere ₹10, oblivious to his pleadings.

'Madam, we don't make much. I have a family to feed. It is difficult for me to reduce.'

Despite her wealth and luxurious lifestyle, the rich lady didn't budge an inch. The poor man had no other option but to agree to her price. Assuming that the vendor was quoting the right price, the lady should have shown magnanimity while going through with the purchase. The very same lady would have walked into a glitzy departmental store, shopped for a dozen items and squared a hefty four-figure bill through the credit card without batting an eyelid. On the face of it, it did not look like an unprincipled negotiation, but it was clear that the lady was exploiting his weakness and taking advantage of his indigence. However, in business parlance, unprincipled negotiations have a different meaning altogether.

Negotiation is a process where two disparate entities with different priorities and goals sit across a table and arrive at a mutually acceptable solution. Ideally, negotiations are aimed at building a lasting relationship between the two parties with accrued benefits for both in terms of business, quality solutions and resolution of conflicts that might arise in the future. However, not every negotiation is successful.

History is full of stories and anecdotes of failed negotiations involving people, corporates and nations; what better example to attest to this than the Partition of

India in 1947, which resulted in the deaths of two million people and displacement of 14 million. The catastrophic impact of a failed negotiation left many in tatters. A single transaction that shook the entire subcontinent could have easily been avoided. Instead, it led to the creation of two independent dominions. More than 70 years have gone by and the wounds have still not healed. The two-nation theory bears testimony to the fact that leaders at that time lacked the necessary communication skills so vital to negotiations considering the enormity of the exercise. Ultimately, the failed negotiation left a trail of death and destruction on either side of the divide. The gulf has since only widened between the two countries. Even as India is taking giant strides to cement its place amongst the leading economies in the world, the picture isn't rosy on the other side. Across the Radcliffe Line, the situation in the deep state is spiralling out of control.

The scenario would have been different if both sides had shown flexibility and accommodation in their approach. Unfortunately, that did not happen and the Indian union was split down the middle.

When two corporate entities fail to conclude due to a variety of reasons, the deal falls through and both parties stand to lose. But the same can't be said about two countries. While one wanted to secede and carve out an individual identity, the other argued in terms of a unified dominion. Quite a few would dismiss Partition as an aberration or an acrimonious dispute centred on religion when it was just a case of failed negotiations.

The three central characters involved in the episode were Mahatma Gandhi, Jawaharlal Nehru and Mohammad Ali Jinnah. Jinnah formally left the Congress in 1921 and joined the Muslim League. From then on, he was firmly wedded to the two-nation theory without giving a thought to the repercussions such a move would have on the nation as a whole. Gandhi and Nehru tried to dissuade him but to no avail; they soon realised that their efforts were stonewalled as Jinnah refused to budge. With barristers on either side of the table, one would have expected cogent arguments and counter-arguments flying thick and fast from either side; arriving at a conclusion based on facts, data and sagacity. Sadly, it petered out into a one-sided affair.[17]

The soft, persuasive approach adopted by Nehru and Gandhi came a cropper against an uncompromising opposition who made a mockery of the negotiations. The Congress and Gandhi then accepted Partition on the grounds that it reflected the will of the people and that it was the only way out. On 4 June, Gandhi, after meeting the viceroy and Congress leaders, said that the Congress Working Committee had agreed to the vivisection of Pakistan and Hindustan, not under any threat of violence but as there was no other option left of getting around the Muslim League. Jinnah was stern, unrepentant and used aggression all the way to emerge the better man. Thus, Pakistan came into being and the rest is history.[18]

Principled negotiations are based on honesty, integrity, flexibility and patience. The Partition is a

[17] https://www.nationalheraldindia.com/opinion/why-did-gandhi-accept-partition

[18] Ibid.

good example of unpreparedness and a lack of strategy leading to the ultimate capitulation of the Congress before the Muslim League. Jinnah was settling for nothing less than Pakistan. Jinnah, a chain-smoker and drinker, was suffering from tuberculosis and had just about a year to live. His illness was hidden from public glare; the only ones who knew about it were his sister Fatima and his personal physician, Dr Patel. The zealously guarded secret sealed all hopes of a united India and helped the cause of the two-nation theory; if the Congress had even an inkling that Jinnah was suffering from such a debilitating illness, they would have procrastinated on the deliberations and avoided Partition.

> Negotiation is a back and forth communication where some interests are shared and some are opposed. The purpose of negotiating is seeing if you can get your interests achieved through an agreement. An interest is why you want something, not what you want. When negotiators start working from the standpoint of interests, they can begin to work with the other party to explore alternative solutions.[19]

While underscoring the importance of negotiations, one should not forget the skills needed to be a good negotiator. A good negotiator ensures a win-win situation for both parties. In the age that we live in, where competition has been replaced by collaboration,

[19] Fisher, Roger and William Ury (with Bruce Patton for the 2nd edition). 1991. *Getting to Say Yes: Negotiating Agreement Without Giving In*. New York: Penguin Group.

a well-negotiated deal is bound to pay dividends to both parties in the long run. The need for structured negotiations is felt all the more when huge amounts of money are involved. In non-life insurance, a few ₹ translate to millions in the long run. Where numbers are involved as in health insurance premium, astute negotiations lead to employees paying the right premium for the right policy.

While there is no one-size-fits-all solution, a good negotiator has an edge if he has good communication skills; crisp, clear communication supported by facts lead to a mutually beneficial agreement. In the realm of negotiations, holding on to your position and showing no flexibility may cost you dearly. A person who is flexible and accommodating can face challenges better than the one who is rigid and obstinate. In the realm of negotiations, 'Let's meet halfway' is a well-used tag line that goes by the nomenclature of ZOPA, or the zone of possible agreement. In simple language, the give-and-take approach will finally lead to a price which is acceptable to both parties. A seasoned negotiator gathers as much information as s/he can lay their hands on and has enough data or more about the other party and the competition. Planning is an important aspect of negotiations. You need to get the best deal for your company.

Courtesy and professionalism are the pillars of negotiations. A deal can never be finalised in a single meeting. A great deal of patience is needed by both sides to facilitate the deal. In the business world, parties take time to arrive at a decision. They regroup, rethink and refine their strategies before coming back to the bargaining table. It is generally after many iterations that both parties reach an agreement.

One can always be assertive without being aggressive. Negotiations are not about being generous and losing out in the process. At the same time, being very rigid and not yielding an inch of ground can drive away the other party. Though there is no place for emotions, negotiations should be conducted in a free and fair manner while recognising the client's right to do business.

Ideally, a successful negotiation is where you can make concessions that mean little to you but a lot to the other party. Your approach should foster goodwill, regardless of the differences.

A good negotiation leaves everybody satisfied and leaves room for future business.

In the Mahabharata, you come across various instances where negotiation skills are on display. The Kauravas banished the Pandavas to the forest for 13 long years, after which a war between the cousins was inevitable. The only way to avoid it was to arrive at a settlement. Krishna thus went to Hastinapur as a mediator. In what could be termed as a fine example of sustained negotiations, Krishna requested the Kauravas to return Indraprastha to the Pandavas. Duryodhan refused outright. Then Krishna dropped his demand for Indraprastha and asked for five villages so that both parties could live peacefully. Let alone five villages, the inflexible Duryodhan declared that he would not yield an inch of land to the Pandavas. In a last-ditch effort, Krishna explained the collateral damage a war would cause. He further went on to say that the confrontation would signal the beginning of the end of the Kauravas and should be avoided at all costs. His repeated attempts to negotiate fell on deaf ears. Compounding the matter was the sightless Dhritarashtra whose unassertiveness didn't help the cause either. Though Krishna's efforts went in vain, he employed every possible strategy, from scaling down his demands to educating Duryodhan on the damages of war.

For Duryodhan, his ego clouded a realistic approach to the problem, which led him to scornfully dismiss Krishna's solutions. His obstinacy became a hindrance to a negotiated settlement. Had he been reasonable and believed in a give-and-take approach, there wouldn't have been a Kurukshetra war.

Negotiations are no walk in the park. Even experts see the need to prepare for negotiations beforehand. The situations calling for negotiations may be varied and diverse but the efforts are always the same. For instance, consider a situation where you have been shortlisted for a job and the company has called you for salary negotiations. How will you prepare for them? If you have no idea what to ask for, you will end up asking for a salary which is far below what the company is willing to offer or run the risk of asking a ridiculously high amount and losing the job in the process. At the outset, your starting salary is the reference point or the baseline. What percentage of the previous salary should be added and how do you arrive at it, details of the company you are going to join and their capacity to pay, do market conditions justify your demand, the cost to the company, the take-home, growth prospects et al—should all be considered as preparation before negotiation.

The meandering river flows around the rocks, avoiding a collision. Hummingbirds burn up tremendous amounts of energy as they dart from flower to flower in search of honey. They are drawn to the flowers which will give them something in return for pollinating. At higher altitudes, geese and cranes make use of the thermal currents rather than expend energy in flight. In the universe, billions of negotiations are going on every second. As you take birth as a human being, your karma determines the life you are going to lead, based on your past. Throughout life, you negotiate your way through challenges and reach your final destination in the best possible way. You negotiate with people, circumstances and obstacles. Little do you realise that you are negotiating with your karma all the time.

15

The Leader in You

> A good leader does not stop until the task at his hands is finished. He rests only after he finishes his work. He is not afraid of failure.
>
> — *Chanakya*

The period is 371–283 BCE. A young man was walking hurriedly through the streets of Pataliputra as if he was on a mission. His countenance revealed a steely resolve even as the fire in his eyes reflected his determination. He overlooked a stump of grass in front of him. He stepped on it, tripped and fell to the ground. Undeterred, he got up and looked at the obstacle that brought him down. Then the man got down to work. He systematically removed every blade of grass in the way, along with the roots. After making sure that the path was cleared, he resumed his journey. Though he was upset, he never let his anger get the better of him until the job was finished, as he channelised his energy in the right direction. He was none other than Chanakya, advisor, friend, philosopher and guide to Chandragupta, the first Mauryan emperor whose sway extended over the Indian subcontinent and beyond.

No discussion on leadership will be complete without Chanakya and the *Arthashastra*—a treatise on governance, leadership and strategy. It outlines the details of the duties of a king and how he can maintain the balance between governance and power while keeping his subjects happy and prosperous. In the fast-paced digital world that we live, soft skills and life skills are fashionable words to use. Business school after business school would let go no opportunity to extoll the virtues of leadership and team building, often quoting professors from across the world. Under the guise of new-age names like disruptive thinking and out-of-the-box approach, we seldom realise that these very subjects were already documented by Chanakya, and successfully applied to practical use as well.

When we talk about leadership, we often talk about world leaders, celebrities, sportspeople, philanthropists and their achievements. There are leaders across professions, in all walks of life. The train driver who stays awake all night and ensures that you reach your destination safely is a leader. The nurse who works in an intensive care unit and attends to half a dozen patients while observing the cardiac monitor is no less a leader. Similarly, a teacher, a traffic policeman and the municipality workers are all leaders. Leadership is a practical skill that an individual possesses, whose work inspires others to follow suit. In the above examples, each individual is doing her/his duty and is a beacon for others to follow. Duty that is discharged with utmost devotion to serve people is leadership.

Not one but a combination of skills and qualities found in a single individual catapults her/him to the exalted position of a leader. A person's leadership comes to the fore amidst adversity and chaos; there is no better example than the story of Aruna Netra.[20]

With their leader in the front, a group of doves led by Aruna Netra was in full flight scouring the landscape for food. Their eyes fell on grains that lay scattered on the ground. As they began their descent, the birds hardly had any idea of what was in store for them. A hunter lurking in the trees had cast a net under the grains and started moving towards his prize catch—the entangled birds. Aruna Netra knew that time was running out. He immediately instructed the birds to use their collective strength and fly along with the net. The hunter rubbed his eyes in disbelief as the pigeons took to the skies along with the net. After following them for some distance, the hunter gave up the chase.

'What do we do now?' asked one of the pigeons.

'Let's fly beyond the mountains where my friend Mushak lives. He will help us,' replied Aruna.

Mushak, who was a rat, got down to work and in a matter of a few minutes, the net was shred to pieces. The birds were ready to fly again. What saved the day for the doves was Aruna's leadership, teamwork, collaboration and above all lateral thinking.

How does one discover leadership traits? I believe that every human being on the face of the earth is gifted with a skill. If he works on that particular skill and makes a name for himself, others are bound to follow. Is there a way to realise your hidden potential, one that will eventually separate you from the rest and propel you to cult status?

[20] A *Panchatantra* tale

Recently, I had gone to a house-warming party. It was an evening of entertainment and fun. Some were preoccupied with singing and dancing while others were engrossed in animated conversations. In a corner was a board with a white paper stuck with pins. Then the host called his 10-year-old son and asked him to draw a picture.

As the guests were watching, the kid took the pencil and checked its sharpness. Soon, he proceeded to the board and began to work. A picture of concentration, he had recreated an entire forest complete with animals, birds and the sun. At the end of the exercise, one could see a stream flowing by against a lush green background with squirrels atop trees, leaving the audience spellbound.

All of us are gifted one way or the other.

How can you be aware of the skills you possess? As children grow up, they tend to display their extraordinary abilities at home, school or among friends. Word gets around and finally reaches the parents through onlookers and observers about the child's special talent. You can even call it feedback. Now the onus squarely shifts to the parents to encourage and develop these skills, else the precocious talent is lost forever.

The idea is to 'catch them young'. As adults, we need to be on the lookout for patterns that can reveal a skill a child may possess. Some kids may have a propensity towards gadgets, musical instruments, art or a variety of other things. They choose an activity according to their liking. As they work in their favourite area of activity, their skill level increases. A day will come when the potential discovered within a child mesmerises audiences.

When people compliment you on your work in an area repeatedly, that's how you know where your skill lies. If nurtured over months and years, this skill has the potential can make you a leader for others to follow.

> *Chanakya believed that leadership rests on the constructs of communication, decision-making, accountability and employee satisfaction.*

> When in the court, he shall never cause his petitioners to wait at the door, for when a king makes himself inaccessible to his people and entrusts his work to his immediate officers, he may be sure to engender confusion in business, and to cause thereby public disaffection, and himself a prey to his enemies.[21]

Extending this logic to the workplace, bosses who make themselves scarce and are unwilling to meet employees of the company irrespective of designation and position will soon become unpopular. Every relationship is a two-way street. It is one of the tenets of leadership. A CEO must meet the employees at regular intervals, listen to their points of view and even implement them if they want to impact the company. This way, the employees will have a feeling of belonging to the company and won't look for

[21] *Kautilya's Arthashastra*. Mumbai: Jaico Publishing House.

outside opportunities. In a way, he suggests that one should keep the channels of communication open at all times. In another quote, the great scholar is of the opinion that 'All urgent calls shall be heard at once, should never be put off; for when postponed, they will prove too hard or impossible to accomplish.'

If you draw a parallel, he is referring to the process of decision-making. Delayed decision-making is a dreaded disease afflicting the corporate world. There are several reasons why it is slow in many organisations. The consequence of delayed decisions may vary from lost business opportunities to shrinking profitability. The reasons for procrastinating are many. In a tightly controlled organisation which believes very little in delegation and devolution of powers, every purchase from a pin to a computer server has to be cleared from the top.

Chanakya says, a good leader should never procrastinate and should make fast and effective decisions. Elsewhere, he addresses what can be considered as the HR functions of the organisation and stresses on the need to keep the employees happy:

'In the happiness of his subjects lies his happiness; in their welfare his welfare; whatever pleases himself he shall not consider as good, but whatever pleases his subjects he shall consider as good.'

Today, we talk about customer delight and employee satisfaction, which are key to the success of an organisation. Chanakya's ideas were in sync with modern practices. He further says that good leaders put the interests of the employees before theirs. He also suggests that greater interaction between the boss and the associates goes a long way in the company functioning as a cohesive, well-knit unit. Leadership is about taking care of your employees at all times.

They weren't exactly the halcyon days. The economic downturn from 2007–2009 had flattened companies irrespective of size and valuations. Lay-offs were frequent and became the order of the day. While the top management burnt midnight oil downsizing the workforce, the axe eventually fell on the employees from the bottom—new recruits, middle management et al.

However, one company stood out. The CEO chaired a meeting with his employees and talked about the gloom that had descended on the outfit. As the pensive employees sat with bated breath, the CEO spoke:

> You have all worked for the company for many years. We derive our strength by our association with you. Good or bad times, I will assure you that not a single person will be asked to leave. We have seen many summers together. We are going through tough times but this shall pass too. Let us rise to the occasion, tighten our belts, sacrifice a bit, take less leave, put in a few more hours of work and give it our best shot to pull it out of the woods.[22]

Within a year, the company was back on track.

[22] An extract of a speech from US-based motivational speaker Simon Sinek.

Relationships are not use and throw razors. What makes them unique is the human angle.

Accountability also finds a mention in Chanakya's treatise.

> Whoever imposes severe punishment becomes repulsive to the people; while he who awards mild punishment becomes contemptible. But whoever imposes punishment as deserved becomes respectable. For punishment when awarded with due consideration, makes the people devoted to righteousness and to work, productive of wealth and enjoyment; while punishment, when ill-awarded under the influence of greed and anger or owing to ignorance, excites fury even among hermits and ascetics dwelling in forests, not to speak of householders.[23]

Chanakya says that performers should be rewarded and the reward is a measure of the outcome or deliverables. If an employee is denied a promotion, it is a wake-up call for him to pull up his socks and show results.

A good 2000 years later, the four skills; management, employee relations, wealth creation and leadership are the pillars on which modern-day organisation and companies function.

History is replete with stories of leaders, statesman, scientists, emperors and presidents and their service

[23] https://quotes.yourdictionary.com/author/chanakya/36839

to mankind. Long after they have gone, their legacies continue to inspire people. Alexander the Great, at the tender age of 12, tamed an unruly stallion known to throw anyone who dared to mount him. The Macedonian monarch presided over one of the largest empires in ancient times. Mahatma Gandhi, the apostle of peace and non-violence, shook the mighty British Empire in India and secured independence for the country. Martin Luther King fought against racial inequality through non-violence. Nelson Mandela brought an end to years of apartheid and racial segregation in South Africa after spending 27 years in prison. They were tall leaders with a legion of followers. They stood out in a crowd. Let's look at some of the qualities of these famous personalities who made a difference to people and the world at large.

1. Honesty: This is a quality deeply ingrained in leaders. An honest leader admits his mistakes and initiates course correction. Emperor Ashoka waged a war against Kalinga. After witnessing death, destruction and miseries he had brought upon its people, Ashoka had a change of heart. He embraced Buddhism and dedicated his life to servings his subjects.
2. Clarity of Purpose: A leader is clear about his goals. He has a good idea of the route and the final destination. He is aware of the fact that it will take him a while to get there.
3. Commitment: Without exception, all leaders have to go through despair and disappointment. What separates the leaders from the rest? They never

abandon their posts and come back stronger than ever.

4. Patience: This is the hallmark of successful leaders. In 1928, Alexander Fleming discovered the antibiotic penicillin. It was put to use only in 1943 to treat wounded soldiers during World War II. In 1948, a good 20 years after it was first discovered, the drug was granted a patent for mass production. Fleming's discovery has brought succour to mankind. To this day, the medical fraternity fondly recalls his accidental discovery of penicillin, the 'bacteria killer', with awe and admiration.
5. Equanimity: Leaders are unaffected by criticism nor will they go overboard celebrating success. They know that victory and defeat are two sides of the coin. They take the rough with the smooth and are aware of the fact that their detractors will see the light one day.
6. Seeing the Bigger Picture: Leaders have a holistic view of things and the interests of the nation. People take precedence over the rest. Their actions benefit many and take the form of a movement. They are selfless and want to serve the community at large.
7. Effective Communicators: 'And so, my fellow Americans: ask not what your country can do for you; ask what you can do for your country' were the famous words of John F. Kennedy. Through their speeches, great leaders strike a chord with the populace.
8. Resilience: Leaders succeed against all odds, even if the world at large may have written them off. Scottish king Robert the Bruce was defeated six

times by the English. Inspired by a persevering spider in a cave, he led his men against a much bigger English army and defeated them, gaining independence for Scotland soon after.

9. Capable of Implementing a Different Approach: Rather than treading down the beaten path, leaders tend to think differently. The British ruled India for nearly 200 years. Mahatma Gandhi used the only weapon he possessed to fight them—non-violence. His immense faith in ahimsa bore fruit as India got independence in 1947.
10. Leaving behind a Legacy: Be it a work of art, nation-building, invention or social service, they inspire many others to reach those lofty heights.

As we turn the pages of history, there is a lot to learn from the qualities of these towering personalities. They were different and stood apart from the crowd. Leaders don't create followers. They create more leaders. They leave behind their impressions on the sands of time. Their legacy is an invaluable gift for mankind.

> *People who work sincerely are the happiest. Most people fail because they just do not carry on.*
>
> *— Chanakya*

16

Change Leads to Success

> "All personal breakthroughs begin with a change in beliefs."
>
> — *Tony Robbins*

It is human nature to resist change and run contrary to the popular belief—if it ain't broke don't fix it. In other words, a system working smoothly is best left untouched.

No system can be stretched beyond a limit. As the load increases with the passage of time, newer demands pile up, exposing its inadequacies. Finally, the machine grinds to a halt, affecting normal production. These are clear indications that the system requires an upgrade or needs to be overhauled entirely with state-of-the-art technology to meet new challenges. In a world that is changing by the minute, we need to adapt to rapidly evolving situations as well.

Why do we resist change? We tend to settle into a comfort zone where everything is going smooth. Why swim against the current when the tide is favouring you? Change is necessitated by a trigger that leaves you without an option. When you move to the west coast of America, you must learn to drive a car on the right side of the road. Similarly, if you are working in Japan, it makes sense to understand the various train lines criss-crossing Tokyo.

Change is incentive-driven. Resistance to change will gradually disappear as you get to understand the advantages of a new system. For instance, if you work in a German company, then learning German will brighten your chances of scaling the corporate ladder. The added incentive of furthering your prospects can bring about change earlier than expected.

Change opens new windows within your mind. It is a gateway to creativity. Inventions and discoveries are all a result of change. Scientists venture into uncharted territory with a positive frame of mind. Their propensity to take risks, irrespective of the results, is an example of change that is worth emulating.

Change stimulates intellectual growth within the individual but what is it that drives change? The urge to learn new things and put them to use in everyday life. Bullet trains tearing down the countryside at 450 km per hour are gradually replacing older versions. The Hillmans and the Morris Minors of the 1960s pale into insignificance against the modern-day Audis and Toyotas. Today's expressways are all about high-tech gear, speed, safety and luxury.

Change is need based. Satellites and wireless communications are answers to the question of connecting far-flung areas in inhospitable terrain when the laying of cables is impossible. Similarly, Wi-Fi provides an elegant and inexpensive alternative to running a bunch of messy cables to a board room with multiple users.

Change cannot be forced upon you. It has to come from within and sometimes, happens in an instant. Habitual smokers have quit smoking after seeing a picture of a cancerous growth in the lungs. For the career-oriented professionals, learning new subjects and adding to his skills reflect their desire to change.

Change also signifies adaptability to different situations. The more flexible you are, the easier it is to change. Change can be brought about gradually by telling people what to expect. If a new email system is being introduced in the organisation, the employees need to be briefed beforehand to avoid the element of surprise.

Change is also about anticipation. Every year during the rainy season, the water level rises, increasing the risk of floods and inconveniencing people. In some cases, water level even enters homes which are on the ground floor.

This time, you are prepared with a pump set to flush it out. In the words of Charles Darwin: 'It is not the strongest of the species that survive, nor the most intelligent, but the one most responsive to change.'

As he was going home, a man saw a butterfly trying to get out of the cocoon. Half an hour later, the insect was still struggling, trying to squeeze through the tiny opening in the sheath. In a bid to help the butterfly, he brought a pair of scissors and cut the sack. To his shock, the butterfly fell to the ground. Unable to flap its wings, the insect was maimed for life. If he had left it alone, the struggle inside the pupa would have culminated in fluids being pumped into the wings, making it air-worthy. We always look forward to the fruits of labour in the shortest possible time. Every process has an incubation period before which one cannot expect results. A healthy chick emerges from the egg after 21 days while wheat is harvested months after sowing. Change happens over a period of time.

A life full of struggles is a blessing in disguise. When faced with challenges, the mind goes into a state of heightened activity, trying to find solutions. Over time, you learn to hold out and not cave in to the pressure. Your confidence is back. Parents who fawn over their children must realise that they are curbing creativity by helping them get from A to Z. If somebody is struggling, don't help them right away. Leave them to devise their own strategy and find a solution. Be thankful for the tough times you face, as they can only make you stronger.

Leadership is not just about change but change at the right time, because the window of opportunity is available for a fleeting moment and it can be a while before you get another. A leader can visualise the future, act quickly and devise a roadmap accordingly. This is, however, easier said than done. Leadership is a mix of confidence, self-belief, creativity and above all, the willingness to change according to times.

We have heard stories of companies who were leagues ahead of the competition in terms of market share and were lulled into thinking that the halcyon days would last forever. What followed was a meltdown and the exalted position was irretrievably lost.

When your business flourishes as a result of a product, the company develops an emotional attachment to that product. The cash cow is seen as a perpetual source of revenue. What they fail to notice is that technology, and not emotion, is needed to be competitive to stay afloat in an ever-changing market. What better example can there be than the ubiquitous Xerox machine that was a permanent fixture in offices and shops alike, available in all shapes and sizes. Unfortunately, the management thought going digital would be too expensive and they never bothered to exploit the opportunities they had.

The Xerox CEO David Kearns was convinced that the future of the company was in copy machines. The digital communication products invented weren't seen as something that could replace black marks on white paper. Xerox failed to understand that a company can't keep making money perpetually by betting on the same technology. Technology becomes obsolete over time. Big is no longer the fashion as hardware is shrinking. All beautiful things come in small packages!

In the VUCA (volatile, uncertain, complex and ambiguous) world, changes are taking place at a blistering pace. The organisations of yesterday are not the organisations of today. Change isn't like a trend or the 'in thing' meant to be a fad. It is a necessity, a compulsion. In the corporate world, we see organisations trying to implement change. Change management is a subject which, among other things, tells us how change can be brought about in a gradual and planned manner.

In these days of mergers and acquisitions, the company that has been bought over and amalgamated into the new set-up goes through a lot of pain.

Employees are forced to quickly adapt to the new processes, methodology, technology, HR practices and reporting matrix. In many cases, the employees are overwhelmed. At times like these, change management helps. The trick lies in taking everybody into confidence before affecting the change. Right from the CEO to the entry-level employees, everyone should be aware of the new environment and get prepared for it. Lectures and training programmes are a must before transitioning from the old to the new. A fair amount of time must be given to everybody so that they get used to the new ambience. If you to force the pace, things might go awry as reflected in the story about the butterfly.

Change management is a process which ensures that transition happens smoothly with the least disruption. Parents have a problem taking their children to school for the first time. The child is bewildered at the sight of new faces—the teacher and other children. Insecurity drives fear and the child yearns to be back home.

On day one, the child refuses to go to kindergarten and on day two manages to stay for an hour. By day three, s/he gets used to the teacher, the other children and all the toys. By the end of the week, s/he refuses to go home!

Change is good. Change management is even better.

Why should we change at all? In a business environment, if you do not change, you will fall behind your competitors and lose your market share. Changes, in terms of implementing new technology, increase your productivity and positively impacts profitability.

One can safely assume that change is success. Successful individuals are always open to change.

They are ever willing to come out of their comfort zone and look at things from a new perspective. They are aware of the fact that for the first few months, the terrain is rough. They also know that as time passes, they will feel at home in the new set-up. Adaptability is the key if you wish to survive in an unfamiliar environment. Be a Roman while you are in Rome.

Successful people have qualities that separate them from the crowd. They never give up even if they may have failed numerous times because they know that they will reach the final destination sooner or later. Enlightenment didn't come to Buddha instantly. As Winston Churchill had said, 'There is nothing wrong with change if it is in the right direction'.

Successful people believe in change and embrace it wholeheartedly. Change can go either way, positive or negative. Confident professionals stay the course in the face of adversity and do not deviate from their goal.

Change impacts our lives in more than one way. It provides us with a wonderful opportunity to learn something new where your creativity, which was probably dormant, got an opportunity to be showcased. In a way, it puts you in touch with some of your skills and provides you with a platform to improve further.

The FMCG (fast-moving consumer goods) market in India will touch a trillion $ in the next two years.[24]

[24] https://www.ibef.org/industry/fmcg.aspx

In the face of stiff competition, companies soon realised that it was just not quality or packaging that mattered. Ease of use, portability and cost were key to survival. Here are three examples that exemplify change.

Case 1: Butter is much in demand in India. It was available as a slab wrapped in paper and packed in boxes. You had no other alternative but to preserve the butter along with the paper or transfer it to another box. It was a time-consuming process. To make life easier for the consumer, companies now offer butter in a plastic container with a lid for storage, doing away with the messy wrapping paper. As a result, the sales of these butter packs have gone up significantly. Away from conventional thinking, this was a change for the better.

Case 2: Hair-restoration solutions are in great demand as balding men try their best to look young. One of the options available was to pour the Minoxidil—a generic medication in the form of a liquid for stimulation of hair growth on to the hand and rub it on the scalp, which was a tedious process. Today, the same bottle comes with a spray, which makes the process easier saving valuable time for the busy professional.

Case 3: Perfumes come in all hues and are a great hit with party lovers. However, they were priced way beyond the common man's reach and the bottles were big for people to carry. The gap between perfumes and deodorants is fast closing. Sensing an opportunity, companies are offering perfumes in a smart 3.5-inch-by-2-inch plastic case for just ₹60, which neatly fits into your shirt pocket. What's more, it is a big hit with college students. Small ideas, big impact.

The fact of the matter is that everyone thinks of changing the world, but no one thinks of changing themselves. You become the change.

Change begins with you. The rest follows.

17

How Writing Can Change Your Life

> 'If you want to change the world, pick up your pen and write.'
>
> — *Martin Luther King*

As a child, I was fascinated with the pencil. This was when I was still considered too young to use a pen. Our teachers would tell us that writing with a pencil would improve our handwriting. To this day, I don't understand the rationale behind it, but the ballpoint pen was out of bounds till the sixth standard. The pencil retained its place, a priceless possession in those times, safely ensconced in the geometry box along with the sharpener, eraser and protractor.

My tryst with writing began at a very early age. I remember the very first essay that I ever wrote was in the fifth standard and it was on a cow. The teacher was impressed and read it aloud in the class. To a great extent, I was influenced by my mother who was a celebrated author with as many as 17 published works to her credit. At 16, she wrote her first book, which was also published. She was a brilliant student with a meritorious career. All her life, she wanted to be a teacher and chose to remain in that noblest of professions till the day of her retirement. Still in her thirties then, she set about improving her qualifications while continuing in her job. By the age of 40, she had a string of degrees to her credit—MEd, MSc (physics) and MA in English literature, gaining distinction in each of them. To top it all, she acquired a postgraduate diploma in teaching English from the Central Institute of English and Foreign Languages (CIEFL) in Secunderabad[25] and passed with flying colours. She continued in the field of education and retired as a lecturer at the age of 58; her life fully devoted to the cause of education.

She translated Pearl S. Buck's *Stories of China* into Kannada and was praised by none other than the author herself. She was also an author of several books and would return to the desk every now and then to scribble a few lines on a paper; ideas that would come to mind.

That was the time when the first seeds of inquisitiveness were sown in me and followed in the footsteps of my mother. 'When I get an idea or a thought I make a note of it lest I forget,' was the usual refrain. A middle-aged mother of two, teaching at college, managing the house and still finding time to write and churn out bestsellers was no mean achievement.

As she continued to write one book after another, she became popular. Accolades started pouring in and she received a lot of coverage in the print media in addition to being regularly featured on television channels across south India. Her crowning glory was winning the national award besides countless plaques,

[25] The CIEFL is now known as the English and Foreign Languages University (EFLU) in the state of Telangana.

certificates and recognitions. She never looked back on her laurels and continued to write. She was the last person to even think of money and never bothered about remuneration until reminded by the publisher. She was the recipient of a national award for teachers in 1983 and the Vijayashree Award conferred by the International Society of Delhi and the American Biographical Institute in 1998. Her works addressed social problems, which included a new approach to teaching in rural schools, and the economic and social problems of underprivileged families. Some of her novels like *Sukanya* and *Sweekara* dealt with abuse of women and male chauvinism. As she was a celebrated speaker and a TV personality, she would often use these platforms to provide answers to problems plaguing the society. Needless to say, she was an icon to many aspiring writers till a few years ago, when a fall robbed her of her ability to walk freely. Undeterred by fluctuating blood pressure and vertigo, her indomitable spirit triumphed over physical frailty. She tried to offer solutions to some of the most intricate problems in our society. Though I could not rise to those lofty heights, whatever I write today is inspired by her work and her passion for writing.

My tryst with writing began in the late 1990s when I was working in an IT company in Mumbai and decided to follow in my mother's footsteps. Right from school, I was good at English and my fondness for the language grew stronger as the years rolled by. At college, I was nicknamed the 'English professor'. As a working professional, I would make the rounds of leading national newspapers after office hours. As most of the offices were situated in south Mumbai, which was close to my office, I would visit them and present my credentials. Since I was into technology, the newspapers I approached allowed me to contribute articles related to that sector. I grabbed the offer and went on to write on topics of general interest as well. My article appeared regularly in papers and magazines. In a space of a few years, I wrote for *The Economic Times*, *The Times of India*, *The Indian Express*, *Dataquest* and *Computers Today*.

Feelings cannot be bottled up and will manifest in some form or the other. What better way to express them than on paper? Not everyone writes, but for those who do, it is a source of joy and a pleasurable experience. Writing is an aesthetic experience, a state of nirvana where the mind is at peace. Writers go through a range of emotions, often searching for ways and means of expressing them. Creativity takes centre stage where the paper or computer screen serves as a medium. A writer reaches out to his readers in much the same way that a painter conveys a message through a collage of paintings.

Going back to the Vedic period, writing had its own set of challenges. Vedavyas was meditating in the Himalayas when Brahma appeared before him and asked the sage to write the story of the Mahabharata. Vedavyas was the right person to pen the epic as he had seen the entire story and knew all the characters intimately. The enormity of the task at hand compelled the sage to look for a writer with exceptional skills. The epic poem running into a hundred thousand shlokas or two hundred thousand verses is the longest poem ever written in history. The task was challenging as the writer had to listen, translate and write keeping in mind the right mix of emotions.

Vedavyas knew that it was an uphill task and sought Brahma's help. Brahma appeared before him and directed him to Lord Ganesha. The Elephant God knew that Vedavyas was capable of composing the epic at a very fast pace. To test the sage, he imposed a very novel condition—once the sage started narrating the epic, he would not stop. If Vedavyas stopped the narration at any time, Ganesha would stop writing and walk away from the whole project. The sage knew that Lord Ganesha, being the god of knowledge, would take down the narration very fast. Though Vedavyas was confident that he could compose the epic quickly, he doubted whether he could match the speed of Lord Ganesha. He wondered how he could ever satisfy that condition when he had a brainwave.

He smiled and asked Lord Ganesha for a favour. He requested Ganesha not to write anything unless he understood the meaning of what was narrated to him. Lord Ganesha smiled and accepted the condition. With palm leaves on his lap and a feather in hand, Ganesha sat down before Vedavyas for the arduous exercise. The sage began narrating the story and Lord Ganesha was equal to the task, writing quickly and accurately.

Whenever the sage needed some rest, he would compose a complicated stanza which was difficult to understand. While Lord Ganesha would ponder over the meaning of the stanza, the sage refreshed himself or composed a few more hymns.

The person who can write has an edge over others. The way you write reveals your persona and people relate to you. In the world of soft skills, verbal and non-verbal communication get top billing. The importance of speech and body language is emphasised time and again. However, written communication is not accorded primacy and is often relegated to the margins.

Albert Einstein had said, 'Try not to become a man of success, but rather try to become a man of value.' Taking a leaf out of the great physicist's book, let us look at the psyche of a writer. Thousands write but a few succeed. How do you qualify to be a good writer?

The only qualification needed to become a successful writer is passion and passion alone. Many writers by nature are liberal-minded and catholic by nature. They believe their outpourings will make a difference. Knowledge is gold of a different kind and needs to be disseminated unlike the one at Fort Knox. By and large, writers share their knowledge and improve the quality of life of every succeeding generation. Their works are a reflection of the trials and tribulations they have gone through, yet retaining that perpetual smile. While leaders impact the lives of many through their speeches, writers influence them through words. They are convinced that they can change the world for the better. Thanks to the digital era, the unending quest for knowledge coupled with the diversity of subjects, every kind of writing will have a reader, somewhere, in some part of the world. It must be noted that readers repose faith in writers and believe in what is written. The writer carries the responsibility of being genuine and dependable. An article once published is in the public domain and there is no way of recalling it. Thousand would have already read and registered it before it can be deleted.

Every time I take a break from writing, I feel a vacuum somewhere deep within me. What I miss most is the interaction with my readers and my followers. A moment can change your life—one song is enough to make you a star; one good piece can get you the kind of recognition you wouldn't have dreamt of. If you are on social media, then your visibility increases exponentially. For a writer or a columnist, the comments of readers are invaluable for the simple reason that they can give you more ideas on what to write about.

After a sabbatical, I returned to social media and started writing about problems faced by working professionals. Since I had spent the best part of my life in the corporate world, it was easier for me to relate to it. I made up my mind to write posts which would add value to the lives of people instead of writing to the gallery. I decided to write frequently and the results were far beyond my expectations. My fan base increased and my followers grew from a paltry 700 to 10,000. Soon, I was invited to speak at seminars and talks both within and outside the country—the high point being the publication of this book.

They say, one thing leads to another and that is what happened. One day, as I had just finished my lunch and sat down to write my post, the mobile started ringing. Even before I answered the call, I didn't think it would be anything other than a routine call. But it wasn't. That call changed my life forever. My readers and connections on social platforms used to read my articles regularly and one of them was at the other end of the phone. He was one of my regular readers and was convinced that I was the right man for the job, which turned out to be one that was to my liking. They had plans to start a company which would offer training, coaching and mentoring and were looking for a senior person to come on board.

After 24 years in the industry, I did not have any intention of taking up a job and was certainly not looking for one. They say destiny lays the tracks on which you walk and here I was, being asked to head a start-up whose mission was to create a world-class ecosystem of elite coaches, trainers and mentors by leveraging the use of technology to provide customised solutions that facilitate measurable personal transformation. I couldn't have asked for more. That to me was the power of writing.

Should you make up your mind to take up writing, here are a few tips which I am sure will go a long way in realising your dream.

Enhance your knowledge by reading the works of famous authors. Develop a style of your own. Include stories, anecdotes and humour. Write when you are in the mood to write. It is important to have clarity on what you are trying to convey through the article.

Data collection and its genuineness establishes your credibility. Pay attention to the theme around which you write. Go through a few iterations before you finalise your piece. Be sure to use available tools to correct your answers. Fix a deadline for finishing the article. The important thing is to start somewhere, as getting the first few lines is always challenging.

No author can write a story in one go. Unfinished scripts cannot lie in cold storage forever. Writing has quite a few takeaways and we will look at some of them.

Writing is lucrative and there is no dearth of avenues for making money. The digital domain is your best friend to spread the word around. In this profession, the rewards are plenty. However, the greatest reward a writer can expect is the feedback from readers, which helps him become a better writer.

At the outset, you have discovered the writer in you. As you write, you keep improving. Someone out there will like your work. Build your following brick by brick. As your social status is enhanced, readership grows. More contacts mean more opportunities and a wider network. You get to meet other writers. Social interactions result in the exchange of ideas, modern trends and current topics.

Try your hand and discover the thrills and frills of writing!

18

The Trojan Called Stress

'It is not stress that kills us, it is the reaction to it.'

—*Hans Selye*

In the days of the yore lived a king who was respected by his subjects. Due to some strange reason, the monarch started putting on weight. The throne had to be redesigned and every day, the royal guards carried him to the court. Matters came to a head when the king couldn't move out of his bed.

The worried minister announced a reward of 500 gold coins for anyone who would make the king lose weight. Physicians and healers from far and near came with their herbal concoctions but to no avail.

One day, a young man met the minister and assured him that he would solve the problem. The next day, he met the king and told him that he had only six months to live. Deeply saddened, the king spent his time in despair at the thought of his impending death. Six months whizzed by and far from dying, his majesty was very much alive.

The young man was summoned.

'For your false prediction, you will spend the rest of your life in the dungeons.'

'By all means, Your Majesty,' replied the man. 'But before that, may I request Your Royal Highness to have a look in the mirror?'

The king was shocked by what he saw. He had reduced to almost half his size and looked slim and healthy. The young man was rewarded. While in the case of the king, stress and worry contributed positively and restored his good health, a top-notch executive was not so lucky.

The technology boom saw many a honcho making a mark for himself in the corporate world. Ranjan Das stood out from the rest. His meteoric rise made headlines. The CEO and managing director (MD) of the German multinational SAP, Indian subcontinent, at the young age of 42, he was featured on national television as a rising star. Educated at Massachusetts Institute of Technology (MIT) with a master's in business administration from Harvard, he steered the company to a position of pre-eminence. A complete family man, he was a teetotaller and a fitness freak with no known ailments. During an interview to a television channel, Ranjan Das confessed that he managed with just about three to four hours of sleep every day.

One day, as he was exercising in the gym, he had a massive cardiac arrest and passed away. Down south, the city of Bengaluru where I live may well have earned the dubious sobriquet of 'suicide city'. Known as the 'pensioner's paradise', in the recent past, the Garden City witnessed a spate of suicides in a span of a few months. Many of them were from the technology space.

The business world with its alluring pay packets has a darker side to it—the untimely demise of employees, possibly due to high-stress jobs. Behind the veneer of smiles, handshakes, suave boardroom presentations and deals, lies a sinister world of intrigue and one-upmanship. The million-$ Manhattans stand tall but very little is known about the stress and strain that employees go through within the enterprise before making the ultimate sacrifice. As somebody rightly said, 'You are a zero if you are dead.'

There is nothing like zero stress and our ability to successfully tackle it lies in reducing it to the extent possible. Stress can be caused by a variety of reasons from anxiety and financial burden to differences and disagreements. According to an old proverb, 'It is better to avoid the slush than walking through it and washing your feet.'

Stress is the body's natural defence against predators and danger. It flushes the body with hormones to prepare systems to evade or confront danger. This is known as the 'fight-or-flight' mechanism.

Stress is unavoidable and everybody experiences it throughout life. What is more important than stress is doing something about it, as a stressful state of mind is neither good for the body nor the mind.

Stress is a misunderstood word and the common misconception is that the word has negative connotations. Nothing can be further from the truth as stress has a positive side to it too. It can therefore be positive or negative stress. Positive stress, also known as eustress, is associated with achievements while negative stress or distress is linked to failure, setback in business or chronic illness. A good day at the office, good news from unexpected quarters, appreciation or positive feedback about training leads to immeasurable joy, a sense of achievement which robs you of the night's sleep. As opposed to this, negative stress like hospitalisation, an unpleasant encounter or humiliation leads to restlessness, increased heartbeat and changes in blood pressure. Different people react differently to situations.

Some months ago, I had gone to attend a music concert. Five minutes into the concert, people were still walking up and down the aisle, trying to find their seats. The commotion disturbed me and I could see my anxiety and stress levels going up. However, that was not the case with the performer who was playing the violin like a maestro. He was a picture of concentration, totally oblivious to the movement below. He knew how to manage stress and master stagecraft.

No state of mind can be permanent. If you are tense in the morning, you will be slightly better in the afternoon and back to normal towards the evening. In reality, you haven't done anything and it's gone on its own without any intervention.

Once, Buddha was passing through a village. He was thirsty and asked his disciple to get him a pot of water from the lake. As he reached the lake, the student saw a cart laden with mud crossing the waters. Looking at the muddy water of the lake, he returned and told Buddha that the water was unfit for consumption. Buddha smiled and told him to try a second time. The confused student came back with the same reply. Buddha asked the disciple to try a third time. Reluctantly, the pupil made his way to the lake. And what he saw filled him with disbelief. The mud had settled down and the water was as pure as it could be. He collected the water and brought it to his master. Buddha smiled at him and said, 'The mind experiences turbulence. Nothing needs to be done to calm the mind. Give it some time and everything will return to normal.'

Thousands of millennia later, Buddha's teachings are relevant than ever. Under stress, we get rattled. Our heart rate increases and anxiety levels rise, making us feel uneasy. But you don't have to immediately start popping pills, take sedatives or rush to the doctor to handle the anxiety. Give it some time and the stress, in all probability, will disappear on its own. In addition, put your efforts to good use. For instance, if you are given a 24-hour deadline to complete an important presentation at the last minute, don't panic. Take some time for yourself to relax and de-stress—go for a jog perhaps—before you get down to burning the midnight oil and completing the last-minute assignment.

Anger, too, causes stress. For a moment, let's look at its medical definition: an emotional state that may range in intensity from mild irritation to intense fury and rage. Anger may also have physical effects such as raising the heart rate, blood pressure and the levels of adrenaline and noradrenaline.

The constant flood of stress chemicals and associated metabolic changes that go with recurrent unmanaged anger, can eventually cause harm to many different systems of the body.

Anger is a Trojan that lies in the system and reveals its true form during an argument or debate, either at the workplace or elsewhere. Anger also stems from inadequacy of knowledge. If you don't have the answer, you get angry. When people disagree with you and they have every right to, you are upset and angry. Control your anger and you would have won half the battle against stress.

In my days of being a tech professional, I was heading the networking and systems group of my company which would provide support to various business units. The support groups were not seen in the same light as the business groups, the reason being that business units generated revenues and we didn't. Sometimes, I would receive unpleasant emails from clients complaining about the service levels. That set me thinking—should I respond in equal measure or hold back my anger?

You can never avoid those unpleasant mails but you can certainly cushion the effect. The moment you get such a mail, never reply immediately. Let your nerves calm down a bit, as they surely will over a period of time. It is difficult to frame the right reply when the mind is agitated. When sanity returns, you will notice that you can reply more effectively while offering a solution to the problem.

Later, I discovered another way of dousing the flames—just pick up the phone and call the person to discuss the problem and find a solution. In the course of the conversation, the person at the other end would have mellowed down enough to listen to you and discuss the problem with equanimity.

The trick is to hold yourself back for that moment instead of lashing out, else the professional relationship may never be the same again.

The first step to fight stress is to try and avoid getting into situations which cause it in the first place. In the course of a discussion, you get into an argument with a bull-headed person who never believes in listening to your side of the story and wants to impose their views on you. The best thing for you would be to diplomatically bring the conversation to an end. Procrastination also causes stress. Pushing tasks to the last minute is an open invitation to stress. It is worth the while burning midnight oil and finish the pending assignment than postpone it. A friend of mine is a serial offender when it comes to catching flights. He cuts it so fine that he heaves himself into the aircraft before the doors are shut. After accompanying him on a few occasions, I have decided to travel separately and extend my longevity by a few years.

At the workplace, deadlines, presentations, travel, the top line, the bottom line, promotions, raw deals are all a part of the mix. I have tried in my own way to come up with a cheat sheet, of things that I should avoid to ward off stress, which I refer to at regular intervals.

Overcommitment: Employees commit shorter time frames which typically is difficult to adhere to for a variety of reasons. They want to project themselves as go-getters and are in a hurry to climb the corporate ladder. Unfortunately, this is an open invitation to stress.

Stress is not limited to human beings. A cheetah, while chasing a prey, runs at 100 km per hour for about 300 metres. As the animal is in hot pursuit, its body temperature rises rapidly resulting in exhaustion and sometimes, death. The animal has little option but to slow down and avoid overheating. No matter how hard he tried, Usain Bolt could not run 100 metres in four seconds. Committing unrealistic time frames should be avoided even if you have to say a polite 'no'.

The Load Factor: This is a typical case of biting off more than you can chew. Driven by monetary considerations, you may end up taking responsibility for too many tasks, often resulting in poor performance and no justice done on any of the projects. This leads to burnout and efficiency drops to abysmally low levels.

Arriving Late to Work or Elsewhere: Stress gets activated when you are late. While catching a flight, some of us are in the habit of arriving in the nick of time. For the upwardly mobile professional, the last-minute entry is probably due to the desire of being fashionably late, but it will trigger an enormous amount of stress, affecting his health.

Waiting: There have been several occasions when I've been kept waiting when the person I'm supposed to meet turned up a good hour late than the appointed hour. Sometimes you are the one who keeps the other party waiting. Such instances of having to wait needlessly can also lead to stress, which lingers on even after the meeting is over.

Noise Pollution: The South Indian city of Chennai wakes up with a bang, ratcheting up noise levels to a 125 decibels as opposed to the permissible levels of 55 during the day and 45 at night. Honking, blaring loudspeakers and industrial noise disturb the peace and tranquillity. The largest democracy in the world has done precious little as stress and tension take their toll on the citizens, especially schoolchildren. It is time to learn a lesson or two from quieter cities around the world.

Arguments: Heated arguments often leave you stressed. The after-effects linger on for days and weeks. Job-related stress may develop into depression especially when the tide turns against you.

Anxiety: A condition most of us experience ahead of a decision which may or may not go in our favour. Business deals, jobs, the precarious health of your loved ones, examination results, among other factors, fall in this category. Bouts of nervousness, laboured breathing, faster heartbeat and a loss of interest are signs of stress.

Having talked about the causes of stress, we need to understand how to counter stress as it may lead to other problems. It is a state of mind that we shouldn't be in for too long. If stress builds up it will lead to a host of other problems like diabetes, depression and changes in blood-sugar levels. So how do we de-stress and lead a normal life? Having spoken to a cross-section of people, I have come up with a list of stress busters that can work.

Music: This appears to be the automatic choice for many. As a stress buster, sportsmen are often seen with their headphones over their ears, listening to their favourite numbers ahead of a nerve-wracking final. Music is linked to our emotions and has a calming influence on the mind.

Writing: People who write can choose it as a medium to express their emotions. Thoughts and ideas find an outlet and the joy is doubled when such writing receives positive feedback when shared with others. Psychotherapy research[26] has found a significant reduction in anxiety and depression symptoms among writers.

[26] https://www.health.harvard.edu/healthbeat/writing-about-emotions-may-ease-stress-and-trauma

Cooking: This is supposed to be therapeutic and believed to help you let go of the built-up stress. Surprisingly, men evinced keen interest in cooking and tried their hand at it, especially when the lady of the house was away.

Recreation: Gardening, farming, flower-arrangement, driving, painting, swimming and a host of other recreational activities are also effective against stress.

Meditation: It is a foregone conclusion that meditation and yoga have brought joy and relief to millions around the world. Yoga's emphasis on breathing and the mind–body–spirit connection also yields strong emotional benefits. People who practise yoga frequently report that they sleep better and feel less stressed. A minimum of seven hours of sleep is essential for the body and the mind to be in good shape.

Sports: A healthy body is a healthy mind. Regular exercise, walking and games provide physical and mental stress relief and can help combat depression and anxiety.

The best way to beat stress is to take up activities that make you happy. Identifying a pleasurable activity is entirely up to you. Keeping the visit to the doctor as a last option, you can keep stress at bay on your own.

19

Public Speaking

> 'If you can speak, you can influence. If you can influence, you can change lives.'
>
> — *Rob Brown*

Back in 2009, Warren Buffet, while addressing a class of business students at Columbia University, said, 'The dividends on the investment you make in sharpening your communication skills will pay off for the rest of your career. Don't take my word for it.'[27]

Almost a decade later, Buffet's words, much like an oracle, have come true. Even today, in fact, for all times to come, public speaking is that one skill that will raise your value by fifty per cent. The kind of visibility and exposure a speaker gets while addressing a gathering from the podium is unmatched. Public speaking is an art that was practised from time immemorial.

Demosthenes, the great Greek orator, was born in 384 BC. As a boy, he struggled with speech impediments. He would often stutter and stammer and had difficulty pronouncing the alphabet 'r'. His lungs were weak and voice, unimpressive. Long sentences left him breathless, making his speeches dull

[27] For the speech, please visit https://www.inc.com/carmine-gallo/the-one-skill-warren-buffett-says-will-raise-your-value-by-50.html

and incomprehensible. A good 2,000 years later, Demosthenes is still remembered, referenced and quoted by modern-day educationists, historians and litterateurs. What caused this turnaround?

Greece was always at war during his time (384–322 BC). Fiery men with vocal prowess were much in demand, to rouse public sentiment against King Philip of Macedon. Oratory and demagogy ensured power and pelf for the ambitious and uncompromising. With an eye on the spoils, Demosthenes began to hone his verbal skills. He practised speaking with pebbles in his mouth and climbed mountains to clear his lungs. Finally, he overcame his weaknesses and mastered the art of speaking. When asked to name the three important elements in speech, he replied, 'Delivery, delivery and delivery'.

Let us look at some of the building blocks that are essential to perfect the art of public speaking.

Today, we have celebrity speakers flying across continents and delivering lectures on a range of subjects. They walk on the stage with confidence, enthralling audiences with their experiences, stories and anecdotes. There is hardly a noticeable flaw as a spellbound audience follows the skilled speaker's every move and gesture, ostensibly through a cosmic connect until the speaker and the audience are one. In this almost all-pervading nirvana, where a powerful orator holds his audience in thrall, everybody sees light. At last, they find answers to the questions and solutions to the problems they are grappling with.

A speaker isn't a speaker if he is unable to motivate the listener. People who come to listen to the speaker are looking for that one spark that will set them back on track, infuse vigour and vitality to face head-on the challenges of life. They look for a new meaning in an otherwise dull and insipid existence. If you can fulfil these requirements you have, as they say, arrived.

In 1893, the Parliament of the World's Religions was held at the Permanent Memorial Art Palace, now known as the Art Institute of Chicago. Amongst the invitees from across the world was an Indian—Swami Vivekananda. There were many speakers and by the time his turn came, it was afternoon.

A distant land, unfamiliar faces and the enormity of the event was enough to make the best of the speakers nervous. Vivekananda was no exception. He prayed silently to Saraswati, the Hindu goddess of learning, and began his speech with the salutation,

'Sisters and brothers of America!'

To these words, he got a standing ovation from a crowd of 7,000, which lasted for two minutes. When silence was restored, he began his address. The Western audience had never heard anybody address them that way and felt a strange kinship which drew them instantly towards Vivekananda. The world came to know about a young monk who brought Hinduism to the world stage, explaining Eastern mysticism in an easy-to-understand manner for the Western world. Later in 1897, he set up the Ramakrishna Mission, a monastic order devoted to the teachings of philosophy and Vedanta.

I have met many people who are authorities on their subjects. They talk at length, explaining the niceties and nuances of the craft with convincing arguments. But what happens to them when they ascend the steps leading to the podium and face an audience for the first time?

The stage is a different turf altogether for the simple reason that a collective entity known as the audience is scrutinising every move of yours. You need to stay the course. The pressure is immense. Be it sports or conventions, the big stage has a debilitating effect on seasoned performers and champions alike.

Sabine Lisicki, a budding German sportswoman, was making waves in international tennis circles in 2013. She created history by reaching the final of the 2013 Wimbledon Tennis Championships and was pitted against the unheralded Marion Bartoli of France. With a big booming serve, Lisicki was the favourite to win the title. What happened was hard to believe. While Bartoli maintained her composure, Lisicki was overawed by the big stage and the pressure started to tell. As the game progressed, she was a bundle of nerves. Fighting tears, she could not get the focus back and lost the match, the championship and the coveted Wimbledon women's crown. Her inability to soak in 'the big stage' pressure cost her the title. What is the solution? The answer, according to me, is a combination of many factors.

Dale Carnegie, the celebrated writer and speaker, made no secret of the effort he would put in before addressing a gathering. Information about the subject, audience, duration and the context is essential for your preparation. Assuming that you write your speech, prepare well and rehearse the lines with the usual dose of humour and anecdotes, you still have some distance to go.

Total command over the subject and the language puts you on a strong footing. However, that is not enough. Remember, the participants are not untried students nor are they uninitiated to display your supreme authority over the subject. Quite a few of them are well informed and are capable of taking you to the distance. They come to listen to you and be entertained in the process. You have to win them over, or else it will end up in a fiasco.

In my experience as a speaker, I could see three factors that could significantly influence the attendees—anecdotes, humour and involving members of the audience by eliciting their responses to questions during the lecture. There isn't a soul in the world who is not enraptured by a well-told story. Your best bet would be to start the address with a story. A story about your failures, initial struggle and the number of years it took to make a name for yourself. This way you would have struck a chord with the audience as they begin to identify you as one amongst them. You are driving home the point that success is no 'press-button operation' and tears and toil are behind every successful person.

A speaker should never confine himself to the four walls of his house. Everyone is a top-notch speaker and an entertainer par excellence in the privacy of his drawing room. But the same thing can't be said when you are addressing a gathering. For many, the stage is an enigma. Call it the dynamics of an elevated wooden platform, nervousness sets in. It is one against two hundred and that is not fair.

This indeed is a case of unfamiliar surroundings. As a first step, visit an auditorium on a free day to get a feel of it. Walk around the stage and deliver your lines before an imaginary audience. Every time you attend a program, get onto the stage on some pretext or the other. Slowly but surely, you will discover that the stage isn't as scary it appeared before.

How do you overcome fear on the podium? The answer is simple. Fear is a toxin, deeply entrenched in the human system. The detoxification process is gradual. Initially, you address smaller gatherings and gain confidence on each outing. A few summers and a dozen podia later, you will notice that fear is within manageable limits.

The popular belief is that an audience forms an opinion about the speaker in the first 30 seconds. Give yourself half a minute more. Humour has a magical effect. If you can entertain them and make them laugh, the first round is yours. Seeing them in splits early on gets you to the next level. Repeat the dose of humour many times during the speech and you've made it through to the end of your speech successfully?

Be sure to never underestimate the audience. You might run into a wise guy in the crowd whose express intent is to needle you with a convoluted question. It is a matter of common knowledge that in every lecture, you find a couple of them. Preparation in and around the subject will help fend off habitual offenders.

So, let's say you are thoroughly prepared with several dry runs. But that is not even half the battle. Now, let us talk about the dynamics of the big stage. The reactions of individuals vary, from the throat going dry to beads of perspiration appearing on the forehead and in some extreme cases, the urge to visit the restroom the moment you climb on to the podium.

This kind of anxiety happens to the best of us. It is perfectly normal to be nervous for the simple reason that you have never been in that situation before. You are intimidated by the sheer number of eyeballs that will be on you. Expectations are riding high and you have to last the course, much like a grand slam five-setter. The margin of error is too close to call. A fine line separates a stellar performance from a disaster. To drive away the initial blues, start by greeting the audience and exchange pleasantries. Tell them how happy you are to meet them before beginning your speech. As the ice is broken, you will feel a bit more comfortable and words will flow automatically.

Modulate your voice, and punctuate your speech with silences to keep the audience guessing. A logical flow, peppered with relevant information, is a sure-fire recipe for a good speech. Soon, the stage won't be such a challenge anymore.

An offshoot of the exfoliating communication-skills tree, public speaking is arguably the toughest of all the various methods of communication. In the digital age of today, public speaking takes a whole new dimension in the social networking space. People are not only searching for information but also the concomitant value attached to a speech replete with ideas, creativity and solutions.

Why do public speakers get such high billing? The truth is that it is a difficult art and comes with a lot of practice. You are in that unique position to motivate the audience and infuse freshness into their way of thinking—be it a career or life. You are not just an expert on the subject matter you are talking about but also the persuasive speaker who can deliver the message loud and clear from the podium.

Public speaking is slowly gaining cult status and once you get noticed, you stand to gain in terms of money, sponsorships and appearances.

A good way to start is to make yourself visible at conferences, events and seminars. Companies and institutions are always looking out for good speakers.

For beginners, get into it right away.

There is nothing wrong with starting small. Try it out in your friends' circle. Take their feedback. Work on areas that need improvement. Read a lot. Listen to erudite speakers like former president of the USA, Barack Obama, author Simon Sinek and spiritual proponent and author Jaggi Vasudev (better known as Sadhguru).

American poet and philosopher Ralph Waldo Emerson had once said that 'All the great speakers were bad speakers at first'. If this not motivating, what is?

I may need a hundred hours to talk about the benefits of public speaking and the dividends it pays. Beyond money and commercial considerations, you have the satisfaction of sharing your knowledge with thousands of people—information they wouldn't have found in textbooks and videos. As you share snippets from real-life experiences, the listener need not reinvent the wheel and would save valuable time in mastering the technique of speaking from a podium.

Public speaking transforms you from a shy introvert to a confident evangelist, from relative obscurity to instant fame. As you speak at events and seminars, your brand and brand value gets established. As you address audience after audience, your network grows and soon you will be receiving invitations from unknown quarters.

In conclusion, I would urge you to get out of the comfort zone and give public speaking your best shot. You want to be the cynosure of all eyes and hog the limelight, this is the right time. Do it now.

Pass through the surly gates of fear and success awaits you on the other side.

20

Use Your Voice to Succeed

'The essence of all beings is the earth. The essence of earth is water. The essence of water is plant. The essence of the plant is man. The essence of man is speech. The essence of speech is the Rigveda. The essence of Rigveda is the Samveda. The essence of Samveda is AUM.'

—*Chandogya Upanishad*

The universe is full of vibrations which, in turn, produced sounds. According to the Upanishads, the first sound ever to occur in the universe was AUM, a syllable made up of A, U and M, which together form the sound Om (where A and U fuse to form O). Om symbolises the sacred sign, the primordial sound and the mantra which is invoked before reciting a hymn signifying the essence of the ultimate reality, consciousness or Atman.

If you look at the three syllables, A and U are produced by opening the mouth and M by touching the lips. The first sound derived from the cosmos was full of energy and all subsequent sounds were permutations and combinations of AUM. Among the various triads,[28] AUM represents energy, purity and ignorance as well as thought, speech and action.

[28] The Vedic interpretation deals with the symbolic interpretation of AUM. Known as triads, they represent an unending list of three.

It is no wonder that sound with its cosmic connection is an eternal concept and the primordial human voice to this day is omnipresent and rules the world.

How many times have you been put off by the person talking to you on the phone? You found that the expected pleasantness was missing and you couldn't wait for the conversation to be over. The person at the other end sounded aggressive and spoke to you with a raised voice. Worse still, s/he was unaware of the fact that s/he was making you uncomfortable.

In the realm of communications, the voice gets pride of place and is the determining factor between a good business conversation and a lifeless one, a motivating public address and a dull speech.

I have attended many seminars and listened to innumerable speakers. Quite a few of them are experts in their respective domains but fall flat when it becomes to talking before the microphone. It is not uncommon to see the organisers of events requesting the speaker to tone down their volume on quite a few occasions.

A pearl is found in the depths of the ocean. Likewise, you spot talent in the most unexpected place. As a trainer, I conduct regular voice workshops where I emphasise the need for a well-modulated voice, along with a few techniques and tricks to bring them up to speed. On one occasion, the audience was an eclectic mix of actors, models, IT professionals, teachers, homemakers and businessmen and women. The youngest was a 14-year-old girl and the oldest, a 65-year-old retired teacher who was fascinated by the audio world. I was pleasantly surprised to note that some of them had a broadcast-quality voice—a fact they were not aware of.

At the outset, I asked them a simple question: Why are you attending this workshop? The answers were all different: A young man wanted to be a voice actor. A 25-year-old was interested in becoming a platform speaker but revealed that her Achilles heel was her voice as she had no control over it. A housewife was keen on taking up an alternate career as an emcee. A young man was all set to try his luck as a mimicry artist and try his luck in films. A radio jockey, a video jockey, a voice-over artist, TV commercials, E-learning, podcasts, background commentator—the list was unending.

While everyone had their own reasons, I noticed a common underlying factor. They all wanted to use their voices to succeed in life. But little did they know that it was a tough grind. The vocal cords are too precious to be ignored and the larynx—better known as the voice box—sitting in your throat—unlocks a whole new world of opportunity that may well become a lucrative line of business.

Voice modulation has an emotional impact on the person you are speaking to. A word or two with the right stress can turn the tide in your favour. In addition, command over the language, perfect pronunciation coupled with the right emotions, gives you that decisive advantage leaving the competition far behind. There is a good reason why we need to modulate our voice. If you listen to a song, the entire composition is constructed on the seven musical notes. The singer starts on a lower note and gradually reaches the higher notes before settling down somewhere in the middle. Imagine a song sung with just a few notes and little or no modulation. After some time, it becomes monotonous and unbearable. It is the same with the voice. If you modulate your voice like a sine wave[29] in the course of a conversation, the listener is drawn towards you, thanks to the intonation and the accompanying emotions which otherwise would have petered out into a dull affair.

Before you venture into the exciting world of voice modulation, let us look at the four basic elements that make up a person's voice—volume, speed, pitch and tone.

When I was working in the technology space, I was lucky to attend quite a few seminars in the USA. At lunchtime, around 300 participants from across the world headed towards the tables where a generous buffet had been laid out. Despite the large number of people, the noise level was well within tolerable limits. I had a similar experience at hotels where there was pin-drop silence even as the 50-odd guests spoke in hushed tones over drinks and dinner. Controlling your volume and speaking gently is the hallmark of a professional and pays rich dividends in the long run.

Be it a boardroom presentation or a speech, one should speak slowly so that the audience has the time to listen, analyse and absorb the finer points of the lecture. Else, what you speak will be incomprehensible and may sound like mumbo jumbo at worst.

The tone is the most important when it comes to voice modulation. It can make or break a relationship,

[29] A sine wave goes up and down and in scientific parlance is called modulation. In speech, when you speak, you cannot do so at the same volume or pitch all the time. When you vary these elements, your speech becomes interesting. For example, a song has high, medium and low octaves which make it pleasant for the listener.

a negotiation, a deal or an agreement. By its very definition, the tone evokes feelings. It represents a range of emotions, from triumph to desolation, from elation to diffidence. The problem with the tone is that it is a dead giveaway and amplifies both positive and negative traits. A warm and friendly greeting is the best way to begin a conversation as opposed to a cold and unwelcome tone.

Voice acting opens a whole new world of opportunities and those who are interested should resolve to utilise their voices to its fullest potential. How does one go about doing it?

The basic qualification to get into the voice world is passion. Albert Einstein once said, 'I have no special talents. I am only passionately curious.' Passion gives you the power and drives you towards success, perfection and excellence. Assuming that you are passionate about voice modulation, the next step would be to prepare yourself for the unfamiliar turf from the cosy confines of your home. So, let's get started.

One of the most lopsided arguments that I have heard is that you will be successful only if you have a deep resonant voice with a timbre. What we hear in advertisements is a voice that is enhanced, edited and beefed up using special digital filters. There is a requirement for every type of voice and timbre for some recording or the other in the boundless voice world.

Voice modulation occurs across languages. Initially, you have to choose the language in which you are comfortable speaking. Once this is done, you have to work on the language in terms of vocabulary, pronunciation, syllables, stress and intonation. Business communication is a different cup of tea and corporate professionals would do well to get familiar with the jargon; for example, words like top line, bottom line, cash flow, assets, liabilities etc.

Just as a sportsman has to be in great shape and pass a fitness test, your voice has to be in good condition for the big day. The first step would be hydrate your vocal cords and avoid dryness. Drinking a few glasses of water or having a cup of tea before a recording works wonders and invigorates the vocal cords. Some doctors recommend hot water mixed with lime and honey, which is believed to clear the congestion in the throat. Just as the body needs physical exercise, our vocal cords should be put through breathing exercises in a bid to exploit the full capacity of the lungs.

At some point in time, everybody discovers her/ his talent and I was no different. Even at college I was nicknamed 'professor' and was hailed as the best English speaker. Coming events cast their shadows and the world of voice-overs was beckoning me. Despite being a techie, I was passionate about media and there was no better place to pursue that than Mumbai. After office hours, I would often visit studios/agencies for voice- over jobs. My areas of interest were documentaries and news snippets.

One day, I visited an agency which was very popular for ads, jingles and dubbing. I was led to a room where the founder was sitting—an old man with sunken cheeks who looked like he hadn't smiled in years. I was led into a dingy room.

'Can you speak a few lines?' he asked, looking at me through his sunken eyes. I did that and followed up with two more narrations in contrasting styles.

'Your English is good. But your voice doesn't have the mechanics. You can forget voice-overs and try something else.'

Far from being dispirited, the old man's words further strengthened my resolve. I continued trying for voice-over assignments at various other places. Over the years, I completed more than 500 projects, from documentaries to corporate films. My films have been aired on Doordarshan, the country's national channel.

For those of you who are interested in pursuing voice-over projects, there are opportunities for every kind of voice and timbre. Somewhere, somebody is looking out for your kind of voice. If not for money, do it for the sheer fun of it. Set apart a few weeks and educate yourself on the basics of voice-over. Listening to your recorded voice gives you an idea about your vocals and the concomitant dynamics. It also sets a baseline for further improvement. For a start, your laptop with Windows or Mac is good enough. A microphone that costs less than ₹7500 just about completes the checklist and can be easily plugged in with a minimum of fuss.

Lionel Messi and Christiano Ronaldo, known for their prolific goalscoring, are forwards and continue to play in that position match after match. Similarly, each one of us has a propensity towards a particular genre. It makes sense to stick to it and not spread oneself thin. A teacher venturing into voice-over might choose e-learning, whereas a mediaperson might concentrate on a genre of voice-over that will complement his career. If you are confident, you can run the gamut across genres.

The genre you choose will be the mainstay for all your forays into the voice-over world.

If you are one of those who is at ease with languages, reading becomes easy. Reading effortlessly is a great advantage for all voice-over aspirants. Speed-reading exercises will help improve your ability to read. Once you can speed-read, reading at normal speed is easy. Try reading as many scripts as possible with varying tempo.

Microphones are impartial observers for every kind of voice, so the first time you record and listen to yourself, it typically may not sound good. The home environment is not conducive to recording and the absence of acoustics adds to the confusion. Clicks, breath and background noise all contribute to what is caught in a recording, resulting in an uninspiring rendition. But don't let that deter you. Practising at home is just the beginning. Fortunately, present-day recording applications have editing facilities. Many freely downloaded audio editors help you offset any background noise and enhance the quality of the recording. Play around with these suites till you get a grip on some of the editing functions. Technology and software using digital techniques enhance your voice to a new level. It makes sense to master these applications and give that professional touch, should you decide to seriously pursue voice for a career.

After spending a couple of weeks working on the basics, the next step is to test your skills in the market. Creating a demo is a different cup of tea. Here you select a paragraph which is to your liking and get it recorded in a professional studio. Your demo is a showcase to the outside world and stands between you and an opportunity. The demo professionals[30] will bring the best out of you, enhancing your chances of landing a voice-over job.

Once you have the demo files, what next? Every aspiring voice-over artist has to cross the bridge to get to the other side. Many websites allow you to create your profile. Matching algorithms will direct you to a prospective client. Word of mouth, personal contacts and studios are all channels you can exploit to get a break.

If you are serious about making voice-over a full-time career, improve your skills at home by recording, editing and listening to professional voices. You can also register for a voice-training programme. Training helps you learn the tricks of the trade and avoid the steep learning curve. Besides pitfalls, trainers will help you make the transition from an amateur to a professional voice-over artist in a painless way. Besides, trainers on quite a few occasions have provided the much-needed break for new entrants through their contacts.

For all aspiring voice-over artists, this is the right time to get in. Patience is the mantra and in all probability, this dalliance will turn into a full-time profession!

The voice-over market is worth billions and the demand is growing exponentially. In India, it is equally thriving, what with mobile phones, tablets, podcasts and television channels churning out programmes on a 24/7 basis.

Every time I conduct a workshop, I am in for a surprise. The participants want to learn more and

[30] The studio personnel like recordist, the editing staff, etc.

make a mark in the exciting world of voice acting. The attraction of the world of sound and voice seems to be irresistible. Making big money is not on everybody's mind, or maybe they keep it under wraps. The emphasis is on learning the art form. Just do your thing and everything else will fall in line.

Remember, your success lies in your vocal cords.

21

The Secrets of Successful People

> 'Success is the ability to go from one failure to another with no loss of enthusiasm.'
>
> —*Winston Churchill*

Once upon a time, a king ruled over a vast empire. He was a connoisseur of art and literature. Learned men adorned his court. One day, he summoned his minister and told him to search for a candidate who would eventually become the court poet.

The very next day, the minister made a public announcement and asked citizens to put forward their candidature for the post. A hundred people turned up to try their luck for the coveted post. The task was cut out for these aspirants. They were given a month to write a book featuring a collection of poems. For the first 15 days, the aspirants were treated to good food and recreation. It was luxurious living at its best.

For the remaining period, they were subjected to hardships of the worst kind—insipid food, hard beds and poor living conditions. At the end of the month, the minister called them and asked them to submit their collection of poems.

Half of them were consumed by luxury and couldn't concentrate on their poetry. The other half found the going too tough when the luxuries were withdrawn. However, one man presented his collection of poems that touched the heart and stirred the soul. He was chosen as the court poet.

The key takeaway from the story is that successful people are not affected by extraneous factors and will not rest until they achieve the desired result. They plough the lone furrow, toiling hard when everybody else has given up. A thin line separates the successful from the not-so-successful category. The former have strong self-belief and don't give up easily. They might seek advice but will ultimately decide what is good for them. They seek information and data from several sources but will take what is necessary for them and filter out the rest. This way they save a lot of time and progress towards the goal quicker than expected. They do more than required and bring to the table a value proposition for their company. In simple terms, they create a niche for themselves by doing more than what is asked for. This essentially means that they are stepping out of their comfort zone and are not averse to risks.

Risk is an integral part of success and people are willing to take risks even at the cost of failing, because they know that failures put them on the right track. The fallout of failure is criticism and you can expect to be stung with barbs from all directions. Failure has no owners while success has a thousand claimants. But there is a class of people who are rarely affected by criticism, and in today's age, they generally take the form of trolls and march on regardless. Another trait that I have noticed is that they go about their tasks silently without much fanfare, as they are aware of the fact that no match is over till the last ball is bowled.

Success needs focus and single-mindedness. Like the shifting sands, the mind wavers from one thought to another and loses focus on the task at hand. Even though you try hard, nothing happens. When the focus is lost, you are concentrating on everything else except the problem. To prove the point, I tried to write two separate words simultaneously with my right and left hand. However hard I tried, I found it impossible. When focus is lost, you are expending your energies on fruitless pursuits. Soon you will get tired and exhausted and will ultimately abandon the journey. This needless dissipation of energy should stop forthwith and focus on the right objectives needs to be re-established. It is not what you are doing to become successful but rather what you are focusing on to become successful. Even the slightest tilt of focus is enough to shift our context and frame of mind from where we should be headed.

The mainstay of successful people is the skill. Be it writing, acting or music, they work on them for many years to reach the zenith. They often test their skills in the market by offering their expertise. You might be the best writer in town but what you are is determined by the publisher and the readers. If your books are not enjoying the kind of readership you expect, something drastic has to be done than living in an ivory tower and making vainglorious statements like 'the world might not recognise me, but still I am a writer who is in a class of my own'.

Let us assume that you have all the qualifications to become a top-notch writer; still, for some reason, you not getting there. It is time to do some soul-searching. Do you need to change your style of writing? Is the genre you have chosen the current flavour? If you are right on your money on both, then there is something amiss. You have not approached the right publisher who has not focused on publicity, so vital to the success of your book. In the ultimate analysis, many factors contribute to success and one needs to explore each facet individually before taking up the assignment.

Successful people are supremely confident but not overconfident. They bide their time and hold on to their position or price rather than taking the first offer that comes their way. They won't budge an inch as they are sure of the value proposition they can bring to the table. These are people blessed with abundant patience and ready to go the full distance. The story of Hollywood star Sylvester Stallone and his rise to fame makes an interesting reading.

Stallone was a nondescript actor often appearing in films as a side character. Educated as an actor, he had a penchant for writing scripts and pursued his twin interests in films. Early in his career, Stallone saw nothing but one rejection letter after another. He could barely make two ends meet with the small roles he got regularly. The struggle with poverty continued for some time and was just about sufficient to keep his family from losing their home. But he never gave up. All the while, his faith in his abilities reinforced his belief that he would make it big in the world of American films.

Stallone was desperate for work, but he refused to accept any jobs outside acting or writing, stating that he was unwilling to compromise his dreams. Stallone even resorted to selling off his wife's jewellery. The family pet wasn't spared either and was put up for sale to put food on the table. Finally, the year 1976 proved to be the turning point in his life. The movie *Rocky*, scripted by Stallone with himself in the lead, was a box-office hit. But reaching that point was no walk in the park either.

As Stallone was looking for prospective buyers for his story, he was eventually offered $100,000 for the script—a massive amount for a man steeped in poverty. The one condition that was put forth by Stallone was that he be allowed to play the lead role of Rocky in the movie. They were willing to bet on his story but considered it a risk to cast him as the hero. Still unwilling to compromise on his dreams despite such a huge break, Stallone turned down the offer. The producers raised the stakes to $400,000, but Stallone kept on declining the offers, insisting that he should play the lead role. Eventually, the studio agreed to pay him $25,000 for the script and give him the lead role. Stallone accepted, immediately went and bought back his dog, and went on to become a successful star. The film, which was made on a budget of $1million, raked in revenues to the tune of $225million. Stallone played the role of the defeated boxer to the hilt, who goes through the rigours of training and finally prevails over his foul-mouthed opponent in a brutal climax.

The film is a true reflection of grit and determination of successful people, not just on the silver screen but in real life as well. The characters of Stallone and Rocky almost seem to merge. The lesson that we can learn from his story is that success cannot be achieved by dreaming alone. You have to work for it, unfazed by initial reverses, till the goal is met. Stallone is still referenced as an example of a person who always followed his dreams.

To achieve your dreams, you need a lot of patience. Patience is a hallmark of successful people. Success is no ATM, where you put the card and get the money. Often one has to wait for months and years to taste success. Quick success will disappear as quickly as it comes.

The anecdote below exemplifies why patience is so essential to reach your goal.

A king ruled over a vast kingdom. To establish good governance, he created the post of a personal assistant and announced that anyone who wanted to apply for the position has to pass a few tests. Thousands gathered before the palace for the coveted post. The aspirants were led to a pond full of water. An old pot full of holes was kept near the pond.

The king addressed the gathering.

'I know for sure that there is no dearth of talent in the kingdom. This is a great opportunity for you to prove yourself. All you need to do is to take the pot and empty the water from the pond. The person who completes the job will be chosen for the post. You must remember that there are a few holes in the pot and it is no easy task. I wish you the best of luck.'

In a matter of minutes, the crowd thinned as the aspirants came up with several excuses and left; most of them muttering to themselves: 'With holes in the pot, it will take a lifetime to empty the pond. I would be better off doing something else rather than wasting time. The king has already chosen someone known to him and this entire drama is being enacted to show people that he is a just king.'

Soon, there was no one left except for one man. He patiently kept filling the pot with water from the pond and poured it on the ground. The holes in the pot caused half the quantity to leak back into the pond. Undeterred, the man worked throughout the day and well into the night. At first light the next day, the man completed the task. To his surprise, a casket full of gold and jewels was lying on the bed of the empty pond. He picked up the treasure and ran to the king.

'Your Majesty. I completed the job and found this casket at the bottom of the pond. Please take possession of it.'

The king was overjoyed and addressed the court: 'My search for a personal assistant is over. I have found the right man and there is good enough reason for it. This man is an embodiment of patience as he did not give up until the goal was achieved. Secondly, he worked against the odds, especially when it came to the leaky pot. Thirdly, he was honest enough to return the treasure. Finally, he completed the task with the available resource rather than complaining or finding fault with the system. From today, he will be my personal assistant.' Patience pays and pays handsomely.

We don't have to look further than the Ramayana for people who succeeded against all odds. Ram had to face hardships throughout his life. Though he was born in a royal family, he was forced into a 14-year exile. He had to leave the palace and spend his time along with Sita and Lakshman in the forest. His problems didn't end there. While in exile, Sita was kidnapped by Ravan and held prisoner in Lanka. Ram and Lakshman were just two against Ravan and his mighty army but Ram never gave up his efforts. He, along with Hanuman and the Vanar army, defeated Ravan and rescued Sita.

The case was no different with the Pandavas who were facing the numerically superior Kaurava army during the Kurukshetra War in the Mahabharata. With the likes of Bhishma, Dronacharya, Karna and Ashwathama in the opposite camp, defeat was staring at the face. Yet they didn't give up and snatched victory from the jaws of defeat.

Success and successful people are defined in many ways. The simplest definition of success, as I see it, is to set a goal, reach the target braving the odds and celebrate at the end.

ABOUT THE AUTHOR

Uday Shankar is a telecommunications engineer by profession who spent over 25 years in the technology space. His penchant for training, coaching and mentoring led him to establish TLRNOW—a company offering high-end training, coaching and mentoring aimed at enabling individual success through transformation in the fast-changing digital landscape for professionals and students alike.

Besides being a motivational speaker, he is associated with the print and television media as well. He has written articles for leading newspapers like *The Times of India*, *The Economic Times* and *The New Indian Express* besides appearing on Zee Business channel as an expert on information technology. He was also a contributing editor to *Dataquest* and *Computers Today*. He loves meeting people and storytelling is his forte. His has wide readership on LinkedIn platform where he writes regularly about the workplace and life skills.